KU-586-567

Maximise Your Mind Power

Improve your mental fitness and maximize your potential

JIM REES

**LONDON, NEW YORK,
MUNICH, MELBOURNE, DELHI**

Produced for Dorling Kindersley
by **terry jeavons&company**

Project Editor   Fiona Biggs
Project Art Editor   Terry Jeavons
Designer   JC Lanaway
Picture Researcher   Terry Jeavons

Senior Editor   Simon Tuite
Editor   Tom Broder
Senior Art Editor   Sara Robin
DTP Designer   Traci Salter
Production Controller   Stuart Masheter

Executive Managing
    Editor   Adèle Hayward
Managing Art Editor   Nick Harris

Art Director   Peter Luff
Publisher   Corinne Roberts

Special Photography   Michael Hemsley

First published in 2007 by Dorling Kindersley Limited
80 Strand, London, WC2R 0RL
The Penguin Group
2 4 6 8 10 9 7 5 3 1
Copyright © 2007 Dorling Kindersley Limited
Text copyright © 2007 Jim Rees

A CIP catalogue record for this book is
available from the British Library

ISBN: 987-1-40531-755-9

ED254
Printed and bound in China by Leo Paper Group

Contents

4 Exercise Your Mind

5 Mind Over Matter

Introduction

Is it possible for people to live their whole lives asleep? Or to be running so fast on the treadmill of life that they haven't had time to unravel who they really are and what they really want. Do either of these sound like you?

Maximize Your Mind Power explores how your mind works and helps you to understand where your beliefs and behaviour have come from. With an increased awareness of your unique thinking and learning styles you can use the exercises within this book to expand your mind power, to stay in control when you are under pressure, and to access your mind power whenever you need to.

> **You'll find success when you know how to look for it**

You will be able to apply the new tools immediately and integrate them into your work or personal life, so that you can tap into your potential more consistently. You'll notice that things that once caused you to lose control no longer have power over you. You will be able to control your mind, instead of your mind controlling you.

The ABC of Success in chapter 2 can be used in any situation to help you gain clarity through awareness, check and challenge your beliefs about what is possible, and maintain your commitment to seeing things through to completion.

By taking a mixture of universal laws and putting them into a melting pot with eastern and western philosophies, this book provides a guide and a short cut to success in your life. You will find some of the strategies for success used by great leaders and thinkers of the past and the present, distilled into an easy-to-use format to help you to realize your potential.

Ultimately, the book's aim is to wake you up to the idea that we all have greatness within us. It will help you to do more, be more, and have more in your life, both personally and professionally. Whether you want to get fit, lose weight, give up smoking, be promoted, increase your ability to concentrate, learn to respond in a more positive way to life's curve balls, or know how to coach yourself; these simple-to-follow and easy-to-apply formulas and strategies will give you the framework within which to achieve your goals.

Assessing Your Skills

These questions have been designed to assess the way you use your mind power. To gain the full benefit, complete the questionnaire twice – once before you read the book and again after you have read it and done all of the practical exercises. The more honest you are with yourself, the greater the benefits you will enjoy.

Before After

1 When things go wrong, how quickly do you pick yourself up and bounce back?

A I expect things to go wrong and I am weighed down by these experiences.

B It usually knocks me down and takes me at least a day to recover and let it go.

C I pick myself up quickly and see what lesson I can learn from the experience.

2 How much personal responsibility do you take for everything in your life right now?

A I believe that I don't really have very much control over the quality of my relationships, weight, health, and general wellbeing.

B I believe that life is a lottery and some people are just born lucky and I deal with it the best I can.

C I believe that life is what you make of it and I take full responsibility for everything.

3 What image do you have of yourself?

A I am usually clumsy and awkward and get things wrong by not being sufficiently careful.

B I'm an average sort of person and I don't think I'm any better or worse than others.

C I am unique and have a great deal to offer.

	Before	After

4 How do you respond to meeting new people either at work or socially?

A I am very quick to judge them.
B I am initially open and will judge them once I have got to know them a little better.
C I accept that we are all different and value other people's perspectives and opinions.

5 Do you set yourself goals in your life?

A I have no clearly defined goals and just let life happen to me.
B I know roughly what I want but I haven't planned it out to the last detail.
C I have clear goals for all aspects of my life.

6 How do you respond to change?

A I don't like change and usually stick to what I know.
B I struggle to adapt to change and just do my best.
C I know that change is a constant and I am flexible and will try different ways of doing things.

7 How good is your self awareness?

A I'm not really aware or in touch with my body or how I feel and I rarely follow my intuition.
B I sometimes pick up on stress within my body and am occasionally aware of how I am feeling and the impact this has on me.
C I listen to my body and am in touch with my feelings and keep them under control.

8 When interacting with other people, how good are you at picking up on how others are feeling?

A I am not very good at reading other people or picking up on how they might be feeling.
B I am no better or worse than others at sensing these subtle changes in people.
C I am very aware and sensitive to other people's feelings and notice any changes.

		Before	After

9 What do you do when the going gets tough?
A I usually lose interest and lower my goal.
B I get caught up in why it won't work and find it hard to focus, but usually get there in the end.
C I focus on what's working and don't give up until I get it finished completely.

10 What pace are you running your life at?
A I very rarely have time for myself, have lost touch with friends, and spend less time with my family.
B I manage to keep in touch with some friends and any spare time is taken up with my family.
C I ensure that I plan time out for myself as well as having a good balance with my friends and family.

11 Are you good at delegating to others?
A I tend to do most things myself because I know I can rely on myself and my ability to get things done.
B I will delegate to people who have proved that they can get the job done to my high expectations.
C I believe that as long as I give clear guidance to any of my colleagues, I can trust them to do a great job.

12 How do you react under pressure?
A I find that I have little control over my feelings and how I express myself.
B I keep a firm control of my feelings and find it difficult to express myself.
C I am completely in control of my feelings and I express myself appropriately.

Final Scores

	A	B	C
Before			
After			

Analysis

Mostly As

These answers suggest that you have little control over the events in your life. You are not very outgoing and find it difficult to pick up on other people's feelings. One of the quickest ways to enrich your life is to slow down and celebrate all of the good stuff. If you want to change, follow the steps in the book and do the exercises (don't just read them).

Mostly Bs

You expect things to go wrong but you hope that they will turn out well, and this means that you are sometimes pleasantly surprised. You have some awareness about yourself and others. Your planning lets you down and you could be achieving so much more in all aspects of your life.

Mostly Cs

You are highly self-motivated and are in touch with yourself and others. You take full responsibility for the things you can control and are well organized. Just make sure that you don't take on too much and forget what is important to you. There's no harm in taking a closer look at your goals to ensure you are still on track.

Conclusion

If this is the first time you have done this self-assessment, then bear in mind this analysis as you read the book. Pay special attention to the areas highlighted by your responses, as well as the tips and techniques – these will help you to reduce the number of A responses next time around and achieve a more balanced mixture of Bs and Cs. After you have completed the book and put the techniques into practice, retake the assessment. Giving honest answers will enable you to get a direct measure of your progress in dealing with the areas requiring improvement – and you will see a big improvement as long as you consistently apply these techniques. Remember that any change can happen in a heart beat and that it will be created twice, first in your mind then in reality. The change you are looking for will be a direct result of what you focus your thinking on, sometimes 3–6 months before the physical change occurs. To get fit, for example, it will have been the thinking and training you did 3–6 months ago, not what you thought and did yesterday.

1
Know Your Mind

By understanding how your mind works and how you store and access information you can start to maximize your mind power. We all have the ability to develop our brains to enable us to do more, have more, and be more. In this chapter you will learn:

- How your mind works and how to access information effortlessly
- To understand your behaviour and conditioning and how to let go of the past
- How to programme your mind and understand the left and right brain
- How to recognize the child within and distinguish between childlike and childish behaviour

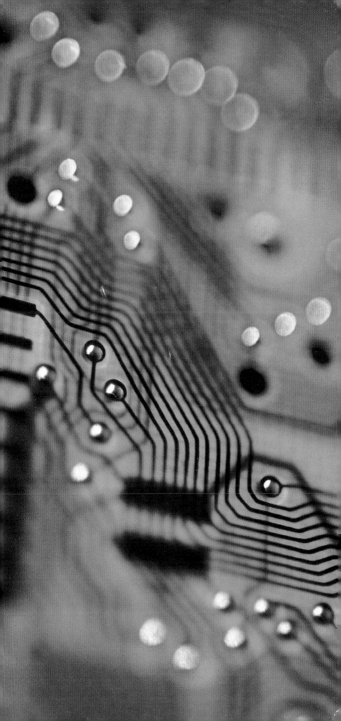

How Your Mind Works

Your mind is like an air traffic controller, taking in information and directing it according to its current knowledge. New information is stored as it comes in – each time you access it, the more hard wired it becomes.

Access Your Information Highway

Access to hard-wired information becomes increasingly easy because of that neural pathway's high usage. When you start linking thoughts together and making connections, your mind lays down a neural network. This is like a busy highway with smaller dirt roads running alongside it. The highway carries the information held in the more frequently accessed parts of the brain, and the dirt roads carry information that is rarely accessed.

What Your Mind Does

Mind and body constantly interact. Your mind regulates your breathing pattern, but you are not consciously thinking about it with every breath. It ensures that your heart doesn't skip a beat, but if it does, it will come up with an explanation of why. The mind's capacity is

Your Super Highway Hard wiring postive thoughts can become a habit. The more cars/positive thoughts you have, the easier it becomes to access.

Accentuate the Positive

Trusting your mind is crucial, but lazy or damaging thought patterns that have become habitual will affect the quality of your life. It is important to learn to recognize these.

→ **Eliminating the positive** – I don't deserve to be successful.
→ **Accentuating the negative** – I will never get over this failure and it will blight my life for ever.
→ **Cutting off your nose to spite your face** – If I can't achieve this one goal, I'll never achieve any of my goals.
→ **Looking at the worst case scenario** – Every minor setback that I experience makes disaster inevitable.
→ **Wishful thinking** – If only the circumstances were different, everything would be all right.
→ **History repeating itself** – If it happened once it'll happen again, especially if it was something bad or disappointing.

seemingly endless. It has the ability to do complex tasks and take in an enormous amount of information:

- The conscious mind can process up to 4,000 bits of information at any one time.
- The subconscious has an amazing capacity and can deal with up to 400 billion bits of information per second.

Keep an Open Mind

Your mind runs your life and has the potential to either help or hinder you in your progress towards living a happy and fulfilled life now. It is important to develop thought patterns that will enable you to maintain a healthy and realistic outlook on life. Try to find the positive aspect of any situation that confronts you. You may be surprised to find that you are able to do things that you thought you couldn't – it is often fear of failure that holds us back.

Think Effortlessly

The power of the mind becomes apparent whenever you perform a habitual but complex task without having to think about it consciously. When you multiply two figures, you are accessing your memory of multiplication tables. You can do this easily because you learned them as a child through constant repetition until you could recall them effortlessly. The first time you travelled from your house to a regular holiday destination you probably had to rely on detailed instructions and maps. If, after many years, you had to provide directions for friends who are coming to stay, you would probably have to think very hard.

Pressure Shot It's not just luck, there's a lot of practice that goes into making the pressure shot to win the match look effortless.

CASE study: Practising to Make Perfect

Mary took a part-time job in a bakery once her children started school. The first time she had to calculate the price of six buns and give change in return for a note she was quite slow in working out the amount and began to worry that she'd never be able to do it. By the end of the day, after serving a number of customers, she had repeatedly done that sum and several others and it had become easier. As a result of continually using the mental arithmetic she'd learned at school, Mary was soon able to do increasingly more complex sums.

• *Mary quickly realized that the sums were getting easier and she was soon doing complicated calculations with ease.*
• *Her new levels of self-confidence helped her to explore other opportunities to learn. She enrolled in a book-keeping course and then started her own book-keeping business.*

Use It or Lose It

We all have days when we just can't recall something we know. Then in the evening, it simply "pops into our minds". If you are having trouble remembering a fact, you haven't actually lost it completely. It's just more difficult to access rarely used facts. A foreign language will become rusty without use, just as your performance on the tennis court will deteriorate without practice. Start chatting in French or knocking a few balls over the net and ready access to the skill will return.

Learn to Remember

Learn to store information so that it will be readily accessible when you need it

Access the information frequently so that you will be able to keep it on tap for when you need it

Recall what you know effortlessly by absorbing any information that comes your way and using it often

Understand Your Behaviour

Depending on your experiences as you grew from childhood to adulthood, you will have learned the basics of right and wrong and will know how you like to be treated and how to treat others.

Hold on to Being Right

The traditional advice that you should treat people as you would like them to treat you doesn't take individual differences into account – race, beliefs and religion, gender, age. You need to treat others with an understanding of how they expect to be treated. Holding on to the belief that you are right leaves very little room for arriving at an understanding of another person's point of

Lack of authenticity shows in your body language

Discovering What Makes You Tick

Being able to unravel how and why you behave the way you do from moment to moment will help you to understand what makes you tick. Consider the way in which you interact with your friends, family, and work colleagues.

→ Line up your thoughts and feelings and ensure that they match up with how you are behaving – this is more about what you do and say and matching your body language.

→ You will know when you are being authentic, as you will feel comfortable with the message you are delivering because it is your truth.

→ You will know when you are not being authentic because you feel awkward. You may not be able to maintain eye contact and will probably fidget more.

TECHNIQUES
to practise

If you frequently find yourself in confrontational or disappointing situations, it's helpful to try analyzing your interactions so that you can understand how and why you behaved and felt the way you did.
Take a sheet of paper and divide in into two equal columns. In one column, write down what you felt about a specific situation, and in the other, write down what you thought about it. Try not to confuse the two

categories and be as accurate as possible.

• Once you know what triggered these situations you will be better at controlling them next time.

• Look at what you thought at the time and compare it with what you think now.

• Try to identify what viewpoint made you feel so negative.

• Think about what this means about you to you – not what it might mean about you to other people.

view. You need to be able to suspend the judgments you might have rushed to make in the past, and to recognize that the needs of others may vary. When you hold on to being right, even when the evidence is against you, you will miss important learning opportunities. You may be closed to the truth because it has been put forward by a colleague towards whom you feel very competitive. Your resentment towards that person will probably stop you from performing at your best, and from tapping in to your creativity. Being able to accept the truth and to forgive others when you feel that they have wronged or slighted you is a very powerful tool that will enable you to live in the present and to stay focused on your strengths.

TIP **Practise forgiveness to enable you to let go of any resentment or anger you may be holding on to in relation to your family, friends, or work colleagues.**

> **What lies between us and what lies ahead of us are tiny matters compared to what lies within us.**
>
> Ralph Waldo Emerson

Understand Your Conditioned Responses

From birth onwards you have had constant input from your parents, family members, teachers, colleagues, the media, and numerous other influences. These have all played a huge role in shaping you. Ask yourself how you became who you are today. The answer to this question is simple – your conditioning or upbringing. Most children grow up thinking that their future and its possibilities are limitless. By the time they reach adulthood, few still have a strong self-image and self-esteem. Along the way, the negative effects of being told "You're clumsy", "Who do you think you are?", "Don't bite off more than you can chew", "Don't be so pathetic", "Don't be so stupid", and other similar things have taken their toll. We end up so conditioned into believing that things aren't possible that we no longer even try to achieve what we may previously have thought was possible. We need to find the key to unlock our belief in ourselves.

Don't Use Your Past as an Excuse

Many people use the story of their past as an excuse to repeat the same outcomes they have always had. They carry their stories with them through life, and everything they do is affected by their negative experiences.

- Do you use your story to justify why you are where you are, and why the quality of your life is as it is?
- Do you carry your parents' story forward into your own life and use it as a reason for not achieving more success in your life?

Past failure doesn't mean you'll fail in the future. If you couldn't draw as a child it doesn't mean that you will carry that inability through life. The same is true of any talent with which you may have struggled while growing up.

Learn From It and Then Let It Go

You don't have to keep repeating negative patterns of behaviour. If you think about the negative stories from your past as great lumps of lead that you are carrying around with you, you will see that they are weighing you down and impeding your progress through life. The longer you hold on to and re-tell those stories, the longer you'll have to wait before you can move on. This does not mean that you should delete great memories from your past, but it does mean that you should think about some of the things that are preventing you from moving forward. You can learn from the experience and take positive steps to make different choices the next time opportunity knocks on your door.

Learn From the Past

Aim to learn something new from everything you do

⬇

Look back at your past and focus on what you've learned

⬇

Apply that knowledge to ensure you don't repeat mistakes

Programme Your Mind

Your mind has enormous capacity for absorbing information. You can train yourself to recall long lists of phone numbers, do difficult calculations, learn a foreign language, or play a musical instrument.

Use Your Autopilot

When a thought enters your conscious mind, it is transferred to your subconscious mind for "filing". Your conscious mind constantly draws on your subconscious mind for all the decisions you make. Most of the time you run on autopilot, doing complex things without even thinking about them. For example, you can drive for long periods through complex road systems, yet find it hard to remember which route you took. Because you have mastered the skill of driving, you do it with little conscious thought. You can learn to harness the power of your unconscious mind by mastering the skills you need in life.

Mind Power Just as a spider can build a web effortlessly, humans have amazing abilities to perform complex tasks without even thinking about it.

Your brain works like a switchboard operator, taking in information, making judgments based on what you believe to be true, and then making decisions. Of the many theories in neuroscience, that of brain dominance is the most common. The brain has two hemispheres, left and right.

→ The left side is more analytical and is responsible for the hard facts, such as mathematics, logic, discipline, structure, time sequences, abstractions, and deductive reasoning. People with a left brain preference will tend to learn step-by-step, starting with the details and going on to the bigger picture.

→ The right side is considered to be responsible for the softer aspects, such as emotions, feelings, intuition, spontaneity, risk-taking, first impressions, sensitivity, day-dreaming, and visualizing. People with a right brain preference usually start with the overview of a skill and then get into the specifics.

Left Brain

OCCUPATIONS

• Analyst • Banker/Accountant • Doctor • Judge • Lawyer • Librarian
• Mathematician • Pilot • Scientist • Stockbroker

STRENGTHS/INTERESTS

• Dogs • Reading • Classical music • Crosswords/sudoku • Logic
• Storytelling • Well-structured projects • Being organized • Rationality

Right Brain

OCCUPATIONS

• Actor • Artist • Athlete • Beautician • Coach • Musician • Park ranger
• Politician • Salesperson • Social worker • Wedding planner

STRENGTHS/INTERESTS

• Cats • Reading for detail • Rock music • Intuitive problem solving • Art
• Acting out stories • Sports • Group work and activities • Multi-tasking

Be Like a Child

When you were a small child, you probably believed that anything was possible. The sky was the limit and you were fearless. Young children are open to everything and closed to nothing.

Listen to Your Childlike Voice

Have you stopped being curious? If you're curious you'll ask more questions and get more information. If you are in a meeting and aren't clear about the direction the company is going in, or you still can't see how the new proposal fits into the bigger picture, then become curious. Ask questions until you do understand.

A lot of childish attributes, such as jealousy and attention-seeking, can be eliminated immediately by using your childlike curiosity. Asking when, where, how, why, and by whom has the potential to clear up any feelings of exclusion and frustration that are common within relationships in and outside the workplace.

Learn to Silence Your Childish Voice

When you find yourself facing one of life's curve balls, it's easy to let yourself get caught up in a childish type of response. By asking yourself "Why me?" and saying "It's not fair" you simply reinforce the problem, and will struggle to come up with a solution that will help you to

Access Your Childlike Nature

HIGH IMPACT	NEGATIVE IMPACT
• Creativity	• Attention-seeking
• Curiosity	• Desire to be king of the castle
• Enthusiasm	• Jealousy
• Fearlessness	• Rivalry
• Openness	• Stubbornness
• Optimism	• Sulking
• Sense of fun	• Tantrums

move forward. You may even end up getting really stuck as the problem **Look for the Positive** By drawing on childlike attributes such as curiosity you open yourself up to new ideas.

becomes bigger – it may sometimes grow so large that it will be almost impossible to overcome. Whenever you find yourself responding in a childish manner ask a childlike type of question instead – "What could be good about this?" This approach will immediately focus your mind on the positive aspects of the situation. Your mind sets to work to discover the positive aspects of the challenge facing you and goes straight to work on finding a solution. Your mind accepts that there is a solution to the problem and looks for the various options available to you and the action you can take.

Life was meant to be lived. Curiosity must be kept alive. One must never, for whatever reason, turn his back on life.

Eleanor Roosevelt

Summary: Setting Foundations

To increase the power of your mind, whether for personal fulfilment, success at work, to enhance social and personal relationships, or a combination of these, you must first understand how your mind works, what has shaped your behaviour, how to recognize harmful conditioning, and how you access and process the information you receive.

Knowing Your Mind

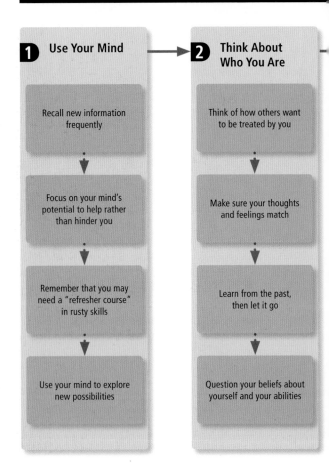

1 Use Your Mind

Recall new information frequently

Focus on your mind's potential to help rather than hinder you

Remember that you may need a "refresher course" in rusty skills

Use your mind to explore new possibilities

2 Think About Who You Are

Think of how others want to be treated by you

Make sure your thoughts and feelings match

Learn from the past, then let it go

Question your beliefs about yourself and your abilities

3 Explore Mind Programming

Be aware of how your mind works so that you can train it

↓

Discover whether you are left- or right-brained

↓

Consider jobs and careers that are in tune with your mind

↓

Look at hobbies and interests that will stimulate your mind

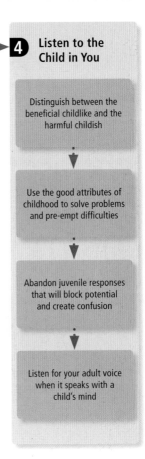

4 Listen to the Child in You

Distinguish between the beneficial childlike and the harmful childish

↓

Use the good attributes of childhood to solve problems and pre-empt difficulties

↓

Abandon juvenile responses that will block potential and create confusion

↓

Listen for your adult voice when it speaks with a child's mind

ABC of Success 2

The ABC of Success (A = Awareness,
B = Belief, C = Commitment) can be used
as a quick check to ensure that you have
everything in place that will enable you to
achieve your goals. This chapter will show:

• How awareness helps you to achieve goals
• Who you really are and how to be
  more aware of others
• How you deceive yourself by holding on
  to harmful limiting beliefs, and how to
  identify and overcome obstacles
  to changing limiting beliefs
• How to use the ICAN strategy to commit
  yourself to seeing things through
• How to use failure as a route to success

Be Aware

It is only by becoming aware of the patterns of behaviour that form the basis of your life that you will be able to take action to achieve your goals and ambitions and satisfy your needs.

Understand Awareness

Awareness is about noticing everything. You need to be aware of the impact of the words you use, your thinking, the pictures you create in your head, the labels you attach to people, the judgments you make about others, and your patterns of behaviour and the impact they have on the way you run your life. It is only by developing your awareness that you will be able to prevent your thinking from impeding your progress towards your goals.

Plan to Succeed

You will need a plan if you are to achieve your goal. Your starting point and finishing point will define the route to success. If, for example, you want to lose weight, ask yourself:

→ What is my current weight? This is your starting point.
→ What is my target weight? This is your finishing point.
→ When do I want to reach it? This is your route to success.

Plan your performance goals as stepping stones and monitor your progress. Break down your planned weight loss into weekly totals. Calculate the exercise you will need to do each week and roughly what your total calorie count should be per day/week.

Opportunity is missed by most people because it is dressed in overalls and looks like work

Thomas Edison

CASE study: Being Aware of Your Needs

A highly valued employee, Peter was a top performer within his company and was asked to take on some extra work. He already worked long hours but began to stay even later to get the job done. Peter's job was important to him but he was a man with a strong sense of family values and he missed spending time with his wife and children. Peter became aware that if he continued this pattern of behaviour he might come home one night to find that his family had moved out. Before matters got out of hand, he decided to delegate some of the other projects to his team, and was soon working a normal day again, giving them an opportunity to stretch their minds and learn. Peter was able to spend more time looking at the strategy of the business.

- *Peter's awareness that he needed to reinstate his work/life balance enabled him to address his problematic workload.*
- *Delegating some of his workload to people on his team gave them an opportunity to stretch their minds and learn more, which benefited them and the organization.*

Achieve Your Goals

Whatever you want to achieve in your life, you need to be aware of the factors that might impede you in attaining your goal. If, for example, you want to become fit and healthy, think of the following.

- What do you eat and drink?
- What exercise do you take?
- What is your daily alcohol consumption?
- Do you smoke?
- Do you get enough sleep?
- Do you get enough fresh air?

Your goal of becoming fit and healthy clearly depends on setting

If you recognize your goal you will achieve it

yourself a series of mini-goals, such as giving up smoking, each of which will have its own impeding factors.

Being In the Now

Being present in the moment, awake to how you are interacting with yourself and others, and aware of what you are thinking and feeling is difficult. Usually there is so much going on in people's minds that they don't listen properly to themselves or to others. They focus on what they are going to say next or are processing something that has just been said. Buddhists acquire the ability to be present in the moment. They practise the technique of slowing down and clearing their heads of all distractions.

Who Are You?

How often have you sat down and thought about who you really are? A lot of the time people define themselves in terms of their personal or professional relationships with others – manager, husband, daughter, brother, mother. It can be reassuring to be able to relate to such an identity – you know exactly who you are and where you fit into the picture. However, when you accept the label that you have given yourself, or one that others have ascribed to you, your identity is shaped by that label and you start to behave in line with that image of yourself.

think
SMART

!

The quickest way to slow down is to notice your breathing – your inhaling and exhaling, and the rate of your breathing pattern.

As you breathe with awareness start paying attention to everything that is going on inside your mind. Ask yourself if you are worrying about something that hasn't happened yet or if you are thinking about all the things you need to do. You will begin to be aware of the quality of your thinking and its effect on what you do and say. The benefits of slowing down will be that your awareness will be heightened.

Find Time to Reflect

Spend time having a deeper look at yourself. This will help you to become more aware of the forces that guide you through your life and anything that you need to change.

Keep a journal in which you can note down all the things that happen to you each day. Ask yourself:

→ What makes you happy?

→ What winds you up to the point where you lose control?

→ What is the person inside your head saying? What type of things do you worry about?

→ What are you afraid of?

→ What assumptions do you find yourself making about yourself and others?

Deep Thinking You can always find time to jot down your thoughts even when you have a busy schedule. Keep a journal with you so that you have something to refer to in the future.

Be Self Aware

Just how in touch are you with your body and feelings, and how often do you use your intuition? Do you pay attention to the signals that your body sends you, or do you ignore and bury your stress? The physical symptoms of stress are often easier for you to detect than any behavioural or emotional changes, which may be more apparent to others. It's important to recognize some of the symptoms of negative stress which, over prolonged periods of time, can cause a complete breakdown in your immune system, leading to various illnesses. Some of the physical effects of negative stress include:

- Disrupted sleep
- Headaches and pains in the neck and shoulders
- Skin rashes
- Changes in appetite
- Changes in libido
- Frequent minor illnesses.

5 minute FIX

Pay attention to your body's stress signals.

- Draw an outline of your body on a sheet of paper.
- Mark any aches and pains you feel when under pressure.
- Rate the pains on a scale of 1–10.
- Identify the situations that cause the pains so that you can avoid or manage them.

Use Your Intuition

When you get a gut feeling about someone or something, rather than using logic to make a judgment, exercise your intuition by checking whether your initial gut feeling about the situation was correct or not. The only way to improve the accuracy of your intuition is to exercise it more. With practise, it will soon match up with the hard facts and logic on which you have previously relied, and you will eventually be able to rely on your intuition to pinpoint the root of a difficult problem. This will help you to achieve more awareness of how others are feeling and will improve the quality of your relationships.

Take Time to Focus on Yourself

Mindfulness, the sense of being present in the moment and becoming fully aware of one's thoughts, feelings, and actions, is a key concept in mind-and-body therapies such as tai chi or yoga. This type of focused awareness helps you to stay calm, centre yourself, think more clearly, and feel more connected to your surroundings. There is no special posture or exercise that you need to learn, it is simply a question of bringing your mind to focus on what is happening within your body and your mind.

→ By learning how to clear the mental chatter inside your mind it becomes easier to focus and push away distraction.

→ When you reach the state of being totally absorbed your mind starts to function more clearly and creatively – a habit or way of thinking you can adopt in everyday life.

Focus on your breathing Place your hands flat against your chest and diaphragm then breathe in through your nose and out through your mouth. Try to visualize the air moving in and out of your body as you breathe. Clear your mind entirely of thoughts.

Focus on your body Lie on the floor with your arms by your sides. Starting with your toes and slowly working your way up your body, tense each muscle group in turn and then relax. This type of progressive muscle relaxation helps you to develop mental calmness and feel more connected to your body.

Challenge Your Beliefs

By challenging your current beliefs about what is possible you will be able to release the brakes on some of the obstacles that have held you back from doing more, being more, and having more.

Take a Good Look at Your Beliefs

People rarely think about where their beliefs have come from. Over time, like a piece of human flypaper, you have picked up beliefs about yourself and your world and they have stuck to you throughout your life. Regardless of where they have come from, your beliefs drive everything you do. It is absolutely critical to your success in achieving your goals that you understand that getting what you want in life depends on what you believe about the possibility of achieving it.

Learning Never Stops Whether it's learning how to use a computer or how to swim, it's never too late.

Beliefs, theories, and opinions are what you use to understand and define the world around you. They make it possible to take things for granted, but can easily become prejudices that remain fixed despite contradictory evidence.

In order to hold on to your limiting beliefs you will have filtered everything by one of three methods – deletion, distortion, or generalization – so that you can maintain your view of the world, the people in your life, and what is right and wrong.

→ **Deletion –** When someone you usually see in a positive light does or says something that you regard as negative, you will probably delete this negative event from your memory because it doesn't conform to your opinion of that person, or your belief about how she usually interacts with others. You may not even pick up the negative aspect because you automatically deleted the event as it occurred. It is as if the negative event never happened.

> Treat your beliefs critically and search for contradictory evidence

→ **Distortion –** This occurs when you distort information that does not fit with your view of a person or situation. Your mind accepts the pieces of the story that match your view of a person or event and changes those that don't.

→ **Generalization –** This is a way of discounting or invalidating information that does not fit. When a normally positive person does something negative, you can still maintain your belief that she is positive by dismissing her action on the grounds that it isn't her usual way of behaving.

TIP Remember that the limiting beliefs that you have about yourself are just as harmful as those you have about other people.

Change Your Beliefs

You probably rarely examine your beliefs and how they have been serving you. You are likely to have become comfortable with your opinions and are not aware that there is a need to change.

Let Go of Being Right

When you hold on to your story, believing that it is true, it's unlikely that you'll ever question yourself until someone challenges your thinking with a different view, or if new data becomes available. The longer you have believed something the more entrenched your belief will become and the less prepared you will be to let it go and move on.

> **Be open to the possibility that you are wrong**

Avoid Being a Flat-Earther

The biggest obstacle to changing a belief is that when you want to hold on to being right, you will defend your view vehemently. There was a time when

References and Experiences

Your reference points and experiences drive your beliefs. If you didn't learn to swim as a child because you were scared of water, you may still believe that you can't learn.

→ The experience of not achieving something when you were a child could be blocking you from attempting other new things in your adult life.
→ The experience of making a single mistake can prevent you from trying again.
→ Your references of other people's abilities may be out of date.

everyone believed that the Earth was flat, until new, incontrovertible data became available that refuted this belief – but there are still some "flat-Earthers".

Fear of Failure

Whether it's in the boardroom or on the playing field, the meaning you attach to failure can be enough to stop you from trying something new even before you give it a go. The truth is that every failure is a learning opportunity. If you think clearly about any situation in which you failed, you can look back at that situation and see what you have learned from it. Instead of looking at failure as a conclusion, try to see it as the beginning of a new journey of discovery. Remember that:

- It is more likely that you will have learned more from your failures than from your successes.
- Looking at every failure as an opportunity to learn about yourself and others and about what to change next time will help you to get the results you want. Life is all about learning.

> **What would you attempt to achieve if you knew you could never fail?**
>
> Jim Rees

Change Your Limiting Beliefs

Look back through your life to explore where you acquired your beliefs about yourself and your world. Then question whether these beliefs help or hinder you in achieving your goal. Look at the references that have supported your beliefs about yourself and whether something is possible. For example, if you have tried to give up smoking and failed, you may believe that it's impossible to give it up.

Empower Yourself

An empowering belief enables you to see the possibilities in any situation. If you learn to identify these beliefs you can use them to balance your limiting beliefs.

- What references help you to reinforce your belief that something is possible?
- Have other people achieved what you're trying to do? If so, how did they go about doing it? What was their recipe for success?
- Have you ever been in a situation where you didn't give up and eventually succeeded?
- If no one has ever achieved what you're attempting to do, what beliefs do you think you will need in order to achieve your goal?

TECHNIQUES *to* practise

Your limiting beliefs may relate to anything that affects you, from your work situation to the types of relationship you have with your parents or your friends.

- Make a list of what you think are your limiting beliefs.

- Ask yourself where these beliefs came from and what references you are using support them.
- Decide whether these limiting beliefs help or hinder you in your dealings with others, then make a decision to keep them or abandon them.

Make Use of Pain and Pleasure

The most powerful way to change a limiting belief is to maximize the pain associated with whatever it is you most want to change. If you're a smoker who wants to quit, consider the damage caused by years of smoking.

→ What is your health and level of fitness like at the moment?
→ How much money have you spent on tobacco over the years? Think about what will happen if you carry on with the habit.
→ What will your health and fitness be like in five or ten years? How much money will you have spent on tobacco? How will your smoking affect your children's health?
→ Will you be well enough to play with your children and future grandchildren? How will your smoking affect the quality of their lives?

You can use the same technique in relation to pleasure to help you change by thinking about the positive aspects of what you will achieve by giving up smoking.

→ Calculate how much spare cash you'll have.
→ Consider how much better your health will be.
→ Think about how much less time you will spend off work or in hospital later in life.
→ Think of how much more time you'll have with your children and grandchildren.

Empowering Beliefs

HIGH IMPACT

- My overall health is definitely going to get better
- My family will give me the encouragement I need
- It's never too late to change
- My willpower is geting stronger all the time

NEGATIVE IMPACT

- My health is already affected so what's the point?
- I have a demanding family who expect me to achieve too much
- I've been smoking for ever
- I don't have the willpower
- I'll never give up smoking

Commit to See It Through

Commitment to see something through to completion is what makes the difference between winning and being an "also ran". The key ingredients of commitment are determination, motivation, and enthusiasm.

Take the Next Step

An astonishing number of people give up trying to achieve their goals at the very point when things are just about to improve. They miss out on reaping the benefits of all the hard work that has gone into aiming for their goal when they may be just one phone call away from getting a "yes", or one extra training run from being a winner. This principle has served successful leaders and entrepreneurs throughout history and it is the biggest gap between success and failure.

Never Give Up Your worst days and your best days all have sunsets, so make the most of every day.

CASE study: Holding on to a Dream

Gina had always known that she wanted her own restaurant. When she left school she took a job in a local pizzeria, and then applied for a job in a restaurant in a city on the other side of the country. In spite of long hours, poor pay, and missing her family, Gina took every chance to learn from the chefs. Her next step was a move to the kitchen of a highly regarded restaurant abroad, but then she seemed unable to progress any further and thought about going home to open a café. In a final effort she decided to enter an international competition and won first prize – a year's training with one of the world's most famous chefs. She was then able to get a bank loan to open a highly successful restaurant in her home town.

• *Gina knew what she wanted and did everything that she could to achieve it.*
• *She kept sight of her goal, even though at one point it looked as if she might not achieve it. Instead of giving up, she took the final step that might enable her to realize her ambition.*
• *Not everyone is lucky enough to win such a prize but Gina's perseverance paid off. Are you prepared to keep on taking the next step when adversity knocks you down?*

Commit to Success

Before embarking on any project, clarify your goals and values, estimate the timescale, and make a commitment to see it through to completion. Break down your planned work on the project into stages and assign markers of achievement to each stage. Assess regularly how many stages you have flagged up and what you can learn from those you haven't. That way, you will recognize the tipping point and not give up just before the breakthrough. When you first commit to losing weight or getting an extra qualification, you will already have made a decision to see it through – there was a powerful positive energy attached to achieving your desired goal, and you were determined not to let anything get in your way. Remind yourself of this when things get tough.

Apply the ICAN Philosophy

ICAN (Improvement is Constant and Never-ending) is based on Kaizan, the Japanese philosophy of daily incremental improvement. The idea behind this philosophy is to look for opportunities to improve any aspect of your life by degrees. Over time, this approach leads its followers closer to perfection. This thinking has been applied in a wide range of industries, from pharmaceuticals to automobiles.

Do It Gradually

Suppose you want to run a 400m race in four months' time. You're keen to win, but you know that you are five seconds behind the pace based on your current track time. Closing the gap in the time available might at first seem an impossible goal. However, if you break it down into smaller targets – a monthly improvement of 1.25 seconds, which is a daily improvement of 0.0416 seconds – the goal becomes more achievable and you are able to measure your progress.

ICAN Model Success is as simple as taking total responsibility and having the right daily disciplines.

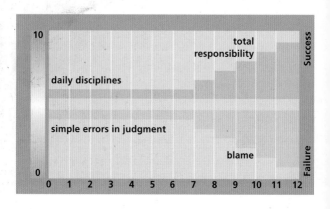

The Knowing/Doing Gap

You probably know how much exercise you should do each week, how many glasses of water you should drink each day, and how much sleep you should get each night. However, while these things are common sense, they are usually not common practice. How often do you find yourself caught out by things that you know you should be doing, yet aren't doing consistently? You need to find some way of motivating yourself to do what you know you should be doing, and to keep it up even when the going gets a bit difficult.

It's easy to do, it's just easier not to. Just jump in and start.

Closing the Gap

If you find it a struggle to make a start on a diet or a fitness regime, or simply cleaning the house, there are ways you can motivate yourself to close the gap from procrastinating about a task to getting it done.

→ The first step is the one that counts. Get stuck into it by committing ten minutes to the task. Once you've started, you'll find it's easier to keep going.

→ Slice it into sections. If it is a large task, such as cleaning the house, just do one room at a time.

→ Incorporate some fun or something interesting in the task. If you are starting a running programme, time yourself and keep a log of how you felt and how far you ran. Then, next time, you have something to compare it to.

→ Keep the end in mind. If you think about how satisfying a clean house is and how nice it will look when you've finished, you will be more motivated to make a start.

Break the Cycle

Using excuses to avoid confronting your fear sets up a vicious circle that is often difficult to break. It's crucial therefore to recognize whether you are using these excuses to avoid challenges on a regular basis.

→ I haven't got enough time.
→ I can't see the point.
→ I always have to do it.
→ I've got too much to do.
→ I keep being interrupted.
→ It's too noisy here to concentrate.
→ I don't know where to start.
→ I'll do it tomorrow.

If you face up to whatever it is you are trying to avoid doing, you will not only achieve more, but you will feel proud of yourself for having had the courage to do something you feared doing.

Identify What's Getting in the Way
When you avoid tackling something, such as seeking promotion or submitting a painting to a gallery, the root cause is often fear of failure. However, this is not always immediately apparent, as you probably use all sorts of objectively reasonable strategies and excuses to hide this fear of failure from yourself.

Fail Your Way to Success
When you were learning to walk, your parents encouraged you to get up and try again every time you sat down unexpectedly. This is a perfect example of failing your way to success, otherwise you'd have been crawling for the rest of your life. Many successful people have applied this strategy, returning to the drawing board again and again to check what had and hadn't worked, to see what they could learn from the experience, and to decide what to change for the next attempt.

Keep a Journal

Most successful people keep a journal to record their own formulas for success. Start your own journal, reviewing what worked well, what you learned about yourself or your project, and what you need to change to get it right next time. When you review your journal, identify your patterns of behaviour on occasions where you have been successful. Try also to identify some of the obstacles that might be getting in the way of your succeeding more regularly. Be honest with yourself about what may have caused you not to succeed on every occasion, and take steps to deal with it.

> Winners never quit and quitters never win

think SMART

Ask "so what?" in situations where you are trying something new. It will make it easier to establish what is and isn't important and will enable you to take more action towards achieving your goal.

Many successful sales people approach new clients with the attitude that some of them will buy their product, and some of them won't, and so what? This doesn't mean that they won't try hard to make a sale in each case, but they won't take it personally if they don't. This makes it easier for them to approach the next prospect. By using "so what?" it helps you put everything into perspective. If you get a "no" you are a step closer to a "yes".

Summary: Keys to Success

Using the three keywords – awareness, beliefs, and commitment – will lead to greater self-knowledge, a deeper understanding of others, and a firmer grasp of how your words and behaviour impact on other people. They will help you to remove obstacles that you are placing in the way of success and empower you to achieve your aims.

Four Steps to a Positive Outcome

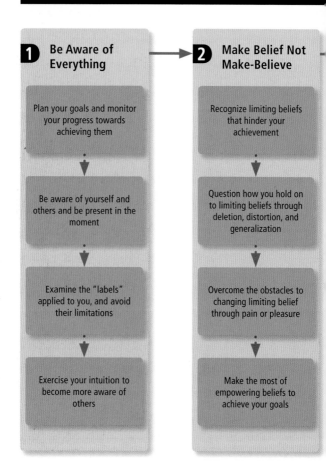

1 Be Aware of Everything → **2 Make Belief Not Make-Believe**

1 Be Aware of Everything	2 Make Belief Not Make-Believe
Plan your goals and monitor your progress towards achieving them	Recognize limiting beliefs that hinder your achievement
Be aware of yourself and others and be present in the moment	Question how you hold on to limiting beliefs through deletion, distortion, and generalization
Examine the "labels" applied to you, and avoid their limitations	Overcome the obstacles to changing limiting belief through pain or pleasure
Exercise your intuition to become more aware of others	Make the most of empowering beliefs to achieve your goals

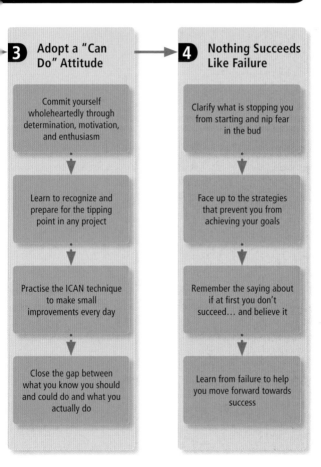

3 **Adopt a "Can Do" Attitude** → **4** **Nothing Succeeds Like Failure**

Commit yourself wholeheartedly through determination, motivation, and enthusiasm

Clarify what is stopping you from starting and nip fear in the bud

Learn to recognize and prepare for the tipping point in any project

Face up to the strategies that prevent you from achieving your goals

Practise the ICAN technique to make small improvements every day

Remember the saying about if at first you don't succeed… and believe it

Close the gap between what you know you should and could do and what you actually do

Learn from failure to help you move forward towards success

Identify the Causes of Failure

After exploring the ABC of Success, it's logical to look at the different causes of failure. If you know what these behaviours are, you will recognize them in yourself and be able to take remedial action.

Recognize Your Triggers

If you think about occasions when anger was your response to a particular situation, you can usually rewind and find the trigger that caused you to lose control. This will often have been an interruption of some sort, or a situation where your courtesy has not been recognized.

- One of your children wanted you to do something or was simply seeking attention while you were busy.
- A colleague wandered into your office to say something of little importance just when you were in the middle of a final calculation.
- Someone's mobile phone rang when you were in the middle of making an important presentation, putting you off your stride.
- Someone edged their way in ahead of you in a traffic jam and didn't acknowledge that you had let them in.

Keep Control

By the time you realize that you have lost control, it's too late. Furthermore, you are probably already berating yourself for an inappropriate response and you become angry with yourself too. Use the A of the ABC of Success – awareness – to help you to understand that anger will not help you to deal with any situation. The energy behind anger is always negative and invariably breaks down relationships instead of building on them. It's difficult to come back from an angry outburst – the memory of the anger will linger long after the emotion has passed.

Boiling over causes collateral damage

Avoid Pointing the Finger of Blame

You should always ask yourself whether you are taking full responsibility for your part in whatever you are attempting to blame on someone else. Pointing the finger of blame stops you from paying attention to your role in causing the lack of clarity. It also prevents you acknowledging that others have played a role in bringing a project to a positive conclusion. Use awareness to lead you to an understanding of whether you've communicated your expectations clearly. You can only do this if you are prepared to take full responsibility for the quality of your communication.

Take Responsibility

Laying the blame on others leads you away from taking responsibility for a problem. If you are late for a meeting and excuse yourself by blaming heavy traffic, you will be missing the point. The lesson to be learned is that traffic can be unpredictable, so if you have an important meeting, take repsonsibility for getting to it by getting up earlier.

Avoid Making Complaints

This final cause of failure is one of the biggest time and energy wasters. It rarely helps you to achieve your goals, and is of no use at all if all you are doing is moaning about something that has already happened. Familiar topics include the weather, traffic, taxes, public transport, queues, speed cameras, poor service, the postal system, television programmes, and the government. It's useful to realize that complaining usually has its origins in the sense of frustration that arises when something is not done

5 minute FIX

When you feel yourself becoming angry, take some time to chill out.

- If you can, remove yourself from the scene of your anger.
- Take a few deep breaths.
- Mentally count backwards in thirteens from 100.

Taking Responsibility

When you blame others for their lack of input or understanding, it leads you down the slippery slope of frustration, which can then cause you to lose control and become angry. How much responsibility are you taking for this situation? Taking full responsibility when things go wrong will help you to learn more about yourself and others.

→ Double check whether whatever is thought to be causing a problem is really doing so.

→ Ask yourself what your input to the situation is.

→ Seek common ground before tackling anything unacceptable.

→ Stick to the point and don't rake up past problems.

→ Think about whether there have been any occasions when you did the thing that you are now blaming someone else for and see if this is why you are so sensitive.

CASE study: Defeating Your Objectives

Daniel had worked hard to save for a luxury holiday for his family and he wanted to chill out and have a great time away from his job. He was so anxious about having a great time that he was constantly on edge and almost looking for reasons to complain about every aspect of the holiday. Because he was looking for faults, he encountered lots of little problems and things that weren't quite right. He complained throughout the first day and, that evening, as he was about to complain about the poor service at dinner, he looked around at his family's glum faces and realized that he was spoiling the holiday for everyone. He decided that he could live with the minor niggles and the rest of the holiday was a big success.

- *By realizing in time that his complaints weren't going to improve anything Daniel ensured that everyone enjoyed the holiday.*
- *He arrived back at work relaxed and refreshed and ready for the challenges of his job.*
- *He used this learning experience from the holiday in his job, and focused on what was good within the workplace and no longer complained about the small stuff.*

to your standards, or when your expectations haven't been met. If you haven't received the service you expected, for example, when you've booked a hotel room for a night, there could be a wide range of reasons for the hotel's failure to meet your expectations. It could be because your expectations were too high, your request was lost, your hotel room was double booked, or you were not specific about wanting, say, a non-smoking room.

- Don't complain about things, such as the weather, that you can't change.
- Even if you think you might change a situation, for example by complaining about poor service, you must remain calm throughout.

Always remember that when you complain about something that has already happened or that you can't alter, you're arguing with reality and can only ever lose.

Stay in 3
Control

Picture this. You are having a good day,
driving along happily, when another driver
cuts you up and you have to brake suddenly.
The other driver is on his mobile phone, and is
completely oblivious to what he has done.
This is one of those moments where you
could lose control, but you won't, because
you've learned how to stay in control by:

- Developing a positive attitude and
  programming your subconscious for success
- Taking responsibility for your choices to
  produce winning outcomes
- Taking four simple steps to clearer thinking
  and greater understanding of others
- Maximizing your performance under
  pressure; minimizing the impact of obstacles
- Building self-confidence and self-respect

Choose Your Attitude

Having a positive mental attitude is responsible for up to 90 per cent of your success in life. So, do you really have a choice when it comes to your attitude?

Take Stock

You can choose your attitude and change it if you want to. First, become aware of whether or not your attitude is serving you well. Grade your attitude on a scale of 1–10, where 1 is poor and 10 is excellent. It's very likely that if you were playing life at a 10 when you needed to, you would end up getting the results you want more often.

Who Allows You to Be Successful?

Are you caught in the trap of waiting for someone to give you permission before you try something new? Do you no longer know what you really think because you are so used to being told what you should think? If so, you need to start looking for what you want in life.

Grab the Moment Every meeting represents an opportunity for success, so make sure the attitude you project is a positive one.

CASE study: Seizing the Opportunity

François and Jean-Paul were salesmen for two shoe companies travelling to a developing country in search of new markets. As soon as François got off the plane he noticed that hardly anyone was wearing shoes. He immediately booked the next flight home. Jean-Paul noticed the same thing and couldn't believe his luck. He phoned his office to tell them that they should consider employing more factory workers to help with the increased demand that he was going to generate.

• *François believed that because no one was wearing shoes, it would be almost impossible to sell any. He chose to play at a low grade on the attitude scale, resulting in a missed opportunity for him and his organization.*
• *Jean-Paul was playing higher up on the attitude scale and all he could see in the same situation was a great opportunity.*
• *The opportunity was all about having a positive attitude and being open to thinking big.*

Stand Out

To be outstanding you have to stand out. Don't hold back from attempting things just because you are concerned about what other people might think or say. Sometimes you have to go against the flow in order to be successful, and that might mean opposing your friends and family. You will rarely get hand-outs from your competitors, whether on the playing field or in the workplace. You are the one who has to put the extra effort into whatever you want to achieve.

Know Your Attitude

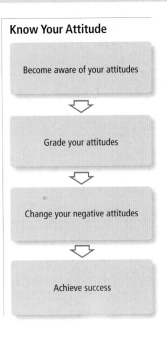

Become aware of your attitudes

⬇

Grade your attitudes

⬇

Change your negative attitudes

⬇

Achieve success

Take a Positive View

The people who seem to be on a roll are those who usually have a positive attitude and expect things to turn out right for them. A strong, "can do" attitude will:

- Help you to move forward in pursuit of your goals
- Allow you to take action
- Help you to identify reasons why you can do something, rather than why you can't.

If you change the way you look at things, the things that you look at will change. If you expect others to treat you badly, you will attract people who do. This will reinforce your poor attitude about your relationships and you will continue to have low expectations of them. You may even start to believe that you are not worthy of a happy, loving, and fulfilling relationship.

Success comes from believing in your worth

What Drives Your Attitude?

Your beliefs are responsible for your attitude and are key to changing it. Imagine a plant: your beliefs are the roots that support it, the stem represents your attitude, and the flowerhead is the result you achieve.

think
SMART

Changing your attitude to your job is easier than changing your job. If you focus on all the good things your job has to offer, it will make it a lot easier to do.

Meanwhile, if you really do believe that your job isn't the right long-term prospect for you, you could be studying for extra qualifications to help you acquire a better job. You might even end up being promoted because your attitude is so good – in which case, your new job might be one that you enjoy.

For example, if you have a strong belief that you should never quit, this will drive your attitude and you

Staying Motivated To learn any new skill may take time, but keeping a positive attitude helps you stay focused and makes the process more enjoyable.

will usually achieve your goals. Your attitude will be healthy and strong and will allow you to regard difficulties as opportunities to learn and as part of the process on your way to success. Your beliefs control how you see and interact with the world, so changing a belief has an impact on your attitude, which, in turn, affects your results.

Programme Yourself for Future Success

Your subconscious mind stores everything that comes into your conscious mind. A conscious thought repeated over a period of time is laid down in your subconscious. Knowing how your subconscious mind works is helpful when programming your mind for future success. If you are always unpunctual, it's likely that your subconscious mind is holding the thought that you are never on time. This thought then encourages you to find things to do that sabotage your punctuality.

Don't Play the Blame Game

You choose how you respond to life's obstacles. Look at everything from your health to your relationships, and you'll realize that where you are now is the result of the choices you've made.

Take Responsibility

Do you blame everything and everyone for why you aren't successful because it's easier than taking full responsibility for yourself? The blame game is easy to play: you don't need any other players, and you can convince yourself that your lack of success is

A negative response won't achieve a positive result

because of the upturn or downturn in the economy, your competitors, your boss, the government, the school you went to, your parents. Do you come up with so many excuses that you don't take any action at all?

TECHNIQUES *to* practise

By getting rid of excuses and proscrastination you will be able to focus on the things you can control in order to achieve your desired outcomes.

If you are not moving closer to your goal ask yourself what is holding you back.

• Make a list of the tasks you are failing to complete and another list of all your excuses for not completing them.

• Focus on what you can do about any invalid excuses that you use.

• If it is the length of your list of tasks that is putting you off, break down the list into smaller chunks that will be more manageable.

• Schedule in a realistic amount of time to carry out each task.

• Watch out for procrastinating tactics and get started on the first job on the list.

Take Control of Your Choices

It's rare to have much control over events that take place, but you do have a lot of control over how you respond to them. This determines the quality of the outcome. The usual pattern is event, response, outcome.

→ **Event** – Anything that happens to you – a traffic jam, a rude customer, bad news, spilled milk.

→ **Response** – How you choose to respond to the event.

→ **Outcome** – The result of your response to the event.

To gain more control over events you need to reorder the model to make it work for you instead of against you, so that the pattern becomes event, outcome, response.

→ **Event** – This will always stay in first position.

→ **Outcome** – Think about the outcome you want.

→ **Response** – This pattern enables you to choose the response that will help you to achieve your desired outcome.

Think of the Likely Outcomes

If you find it difficult to think about the outcome you want before responding to an event, it may help to think about the outcome you don't want. Ask yourself what the outcome would be if you responded in different ways, and whether that would be desirable. For example, if you respond with anger, you might lose control, your blood pressure will shoot up, and you will be less effective for the rest of the day. If you respond negatively, you will be closing off the possibility of exploring ways of turning the event around to achieve a positive outcome. If you blame others for a negative outcome they will be unwilling to help you to improve the situation. Worrying about a situation without taking practical steps to retrieve it will achieve nothing except elevated stress levels.

Play the Results Game

Are you prepared to do whatever it takes to live your destiny, to keep on going against the odds and against the flow? How many times will you get back up and dust yourself off to have another go at living your destiny? When things aren't going so well in your life, and there's an obstacle around every corner, life may appear to be easier for everyone else. However, all the things that have the potential to derail you on your way to success apply equally to other people who have already achieved great success in their lives. They will have had to overcome various obstacles on their way to achieving their goals.

CASE study: Hitting the Pause Button

Rona was driving along the motorway in a positive frame of mind, ready for her meeting with a new client. When she hit a tailback that clearly wasn't going to move for a while, her initial response was to become stressed and worry about being late for her meeting. She quickly realized that this wasn't a resourceful frame of mind, focused on the outcome she wanted from the meeting, and began to think about what she could do to salvage the situation. She phoned Sonya, her new client, to explain what had happened. While she sat in the car she took steps to shorten her presentation so that it would take less time to deliver. When she arrived at the meeting she was calm and collected and made such a good presentation that she gained the new business she wanted.

- *By amending her initial reaction to an event over which she had no control, Rona was able to maintain her professionalism and make a good impression.*
- *By keeping her focus she achieved the outcome she wanted and gained some valuable new business.*

Make Yourself a Winner

Think about the people you know or admire who have achieved success in their lives and you'll realize that there's something special about winners.

→ Winners achieve more in their lives because they step up and say yes more often.

→ Winners look for opportunities in every situation.

→ Winners have a radar set to seek out things that will take them towards their goals.

→ Winners remain in a constant state of being open and ready.

If you want to be a winner, you must recognize that when you take aim, you might not get the exact result you want. However, you will get a result – the key is to adjust your aim from that new position. You may need to adjust in this way many times before you get the results you are looking for in your life.

Embrace Success Whether it's getting a degree or achieving another long term goal, don't allow minor setbacks to derail your objective.

Slow Down and Take Stock

Life is lived at such a pace that we rarely look forward to check that we are heading in the right direction. Many useful lessons are missed out, concealed by the busyness of our daily grind.

Curb the Karoshi

The Japanese have a new word for a recent phenomenon – *karoshi*, meaning death by overwork. The pressure to do more with less gives rise to stress and depression and time off work. This increases the pressure on those left to carry the extra workload. Excessive stress depresses the immune system and people are no longer able to resist the viruses that circulate in offices. Sick leave puts even more pressure on those left to hold the fort.

Slow Down and Pay Attention

When you're having a conversation, do you ever find yourself formulating your response when you should be listening to the other person? You probably miss a lot of what is being said because you're busy coming up with your own argument while he is still speaking. Pay attention to body language and the pace and tone of what is being said, and watch how other people in the group are responding to the person who is speaking.

Use the SLOW Model

Slow down and pay attention to what other people are saying to you

Listen to your self talk and challenge it if you think that what it is telling you is untrue

Organize your thoughts by asking questions to clarify anything you're not sure about

Work out how to respond in the most appropriate way so that you will make a good impression

Check Out Your Listening Levels

There are five basic levels of listening. Knowing these will help you gauge where you are next time you are having a conversation.

- **Level 1** – Ignoring the speaker
- **Level 2** – Pretending to listen
- **Level 3** – Selective listening
- **Level 4** – Attentive listening
- **Level 5** – Empathic listening

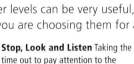

For fast-acting relief from stress, slow down

These are all self-explanatory and highlight not only that it takes a strong awareness to get to levels 4 and 5, but also that a lot of information can be lost at the lower levels. There are times, of course, when the three lower levels can be very useful, as long as you are aware that you are choosing them for a specific purpose – for example, levels 1–3 to block out anger.

Stop, Look and Listen Taking the time out to pay attention to the speaker is key to effective listening.

Listen to Your Self Talk

You spend more time talking to yourself than to any other person. Your internal voice is also your inner critic and is responsible when you jump to conclusions and make assumptions about what someone else is saying. Your inner critic will leap to a negative conclusion, assuming, for example, that the person speaking is trying to make you look bad within the team. Your inner critic jumps in to say, "Of course he would say this about me. He's trying to make me look bad in front of everyone and blame me for the delays." This conclusion may well be false, and your poor judgment of a situation can cause you to waste a lot of energy. Challenge your self talk by asking "Is that true?" This will enable you to suspend judgment and keep an open mind.

Think before responding to your inner voice

Organize Your Thoughts

You are now in a better position to organize your thoughts. You might want to ask questions to gain greater clarity before coming up with your response. The fact that you have listened properly puts you in a better position to contribute to the process. Others around you will see that you encourage people to speak and share their views, which allows for a more open dialogue within the team or with an individual.

Work Out How to Respond

Now that you have gone through the process of slowing down, listening at levels 4 and 5, have taken account of your own self talk, and had time to organize your thoughts, you can respond in the most appropriate way. Working out how to respond becomes almost effortless. Because you have given someone your full attention and stayed in the moment, listening and engaged, he will be

TECHNIQUES
to practise

From time to time, especially following an inconclusive or unsuccessful meeting or an acrimonious conversation, make yourself a SLOW score card.

Award yourself one point for each time you did one of the following things:

- Finished someone's sentence for him, assuming you knew what he was going to say
- Interrupted someone while he was still speaking
- Looked at your watch and didn't pay attention
- Didn't take time to organize your thoughts
- Started speaking as soon as the person speaking to you paused for breath
- Started speaking about a completely different topic from that being discussed
- Jumped to your own defence when no one had accused you of anything
- Gave the impression, through your body language, that you were going to do any of these things, thus destroying someone's train of thought.

well disposed to hear your point of view and be more accepting of what you have to say. If you look at the universal law of cause and effect in the context of your interactions with others, you will see how important it is to slow down and take notice of what you are doing. The fourth step in the SLOW model is the way in which you respond, and this could be the opportunity to make a positive impression. The more often you use each step in the SLOW model, the more you will find that you are able to add value to each conversation that you have. With a heightened awareness of where the other person is coming from, you will be able to respond appropriately.

> **I have lived a long life and had many troubles, most of which never happened.**
>
> Mark Twain

Perform Well Under Pressure

The ability to perform under pressure is a key element in the difference between a nightmare and a dream come true. Knowing what underpins your best performance and what gets in its way is crucial.

What's Getting in Your Way?

You start out each day with 100 per cent of your potential. If you could hold on to that, you would be able to handle most of the challenges that come your way. However, things always happen through the day to interfere with your performance, eating away at your percentage. Your actual performance can therefore be seen as your potential minus the interferences that occur through your day.

Potential — Interference = Performance

Reduce the Interferences

Make a list of all of the interferences that you could encounter during your day. This might include e-mails, phone calls, text messages, interruptions by colleagues, overrunning meetings, meetings starting late. Your own thinking can also get in the way. Take action to do something about each of the interferences to minimize the impact they have on you. You could, for example, decide to read your e-mails only once an hour, and to respond only to those that require a response. If you're working on something that requires your concentration, switch your phone over to voicemail for 30 minutes. Simple things like this will make all the difference to your performance.

TIP If the best time to plant a tree was 20 years ago, the next best time is now. Close the gap between what is important to you and how you use your time.

Don't Try to Do Too Much

If you accept that you can do only one thing effectively at a time, you'll be able to complete tasks with greater focus and energy. Avoid doing several things, but none of them well.

Talking but Failing to Communicate
Talking on the phone while simultaneously writing an e-mail will result in neither a great conversation nor a message that makes complete sense. Do one thing or the other.

Hearing but Not Listening
Because you are distracted you are not giving your full attention to the conversation, and before you press the send button you are likely to discover a mass of mistakes on screen.

Making Mistakes You'll Regret
Even worse, you may send the e-mail, unaware of the errors and spelling mistakes until you get a reply. Multi-tasking in such circumstances is to the benefit of no one.

Delete Worry

If you spend a lot of your time focused on and worrying about things that might happen or could happen, yet hardly ever do, you need to come up with an alternative approach. Otherwise you will follow this fruitless pattern of behaviour for the rest of your life.

Re-Frame Your Thinking

Imagine that your car has broken down so you can't drive to the supermarket as planned. Rather than worry that you won't be able to cook dinner for the family, try re-framing your worry into critical thinking. See if you can come up with some other options.

- Ask a friend to drive you to the supermarket.
- Ask another member of the family to pick up something quick to cook on the way home from work.
- Borrow something from a neighbour.
- Order a delivery online.
- Find something in the freezer that you could thaw quickly.

Look for the Positive Focus on the bright side of life and you will save countless precious hours worrying about things that might never happen.

CASE study: Looking on the Bright Side

Enrico bragged about his worrying strategy – he'd tell his friends that whenever he worried about a possible bad outcome, the bad outcome usually never happened! His way of looking at life was to expect the worst and hope for the best – that way he could never be disappointed. Also, early in his career he had a few setbacks that he chose to carry forward, and this became part of his thinking.

A friend pointed out that Enrico's approach was ensuring that he would miss opportunities and fail to achieve his true potential. Enrico thought about what his friend said and decided that he would try in future to expect the best. He had always wanted to start his own business and six months after he changed his strategy he seized an opportunity to set up on his own.

- *Enrico's worrying strategy had prevented him from dreaming big and led to him missing out on life's opportunities.*
- *His new positive attitude meant that he was willing to try things that carried some element of risk.*
- *His improved outlook on life had the bonus of improving his prospects and his quality of life.*
- *If you were to look on the bright side, what opportunities might you see and take as a result of your new perspective?*

Once you have done the critical thinking you can take action and stop worrying. This way of re-framing your thinking works with even vaguer worries. If you find yourself thinking about the consequences if something dreadful happened, simply apply the critical thinking strategy to come up with options for dealing with it. Then, with a plan in place, you can return to the present and focus on the things that are important now.

Obliterate Guilt

Another factor that takes you away from the "now" is guilt. You worry about not having done something, and that helps to pile on the guilt. This pattern of behaviour can make you feel so helpless that you fail to take any action at all. Banish guilt from your life.

Act As If It Were Possible

If you are seeking promotion, want to start saving money for a particular purpose, or plan to improve your golf swing, act as if were possible. This will give you the confidence to make it happen.

Focus on the Possibilities

When you act as if something were possible you start focusing on it and begin to behave as if it the event had actually happened. For example, you decide that you want to be promoted at work, so you look for opportunities that you might have missed if you weren't focused on promotion as a probability. When you start acting as if something were possible you begin to send messages to your mind that you are seeking promotion,

Your past does not dictate your future

TECHNIQUES *to* practise

Try to apply positive rather than negative labels to yourself and others.
Think about what you would see if you thought about others in terms of their potential and in a positive light.

- Make a list of all of your family members, friends, and work colleagues.
- Write down what you think they are good at and the things that you think they're not so good at.

- Ask yourself whether your opinion of them is fair – could you have been wrong in your assessment, or could they have changed or developed?
- Decide that in future you will challenge any labels before you apply them to yourself or to others.
- Start looking for opportunities to give positive feedback.
- Accept the gift of positive feedback from others, and thank them for it.

with the result that you start dressing, talking, feeling, and thinking as if you were already the person you would be if you were doing that new job. This positive and focused behaviour will set you up for success, other people will notice that you are more upbeat and enthusiastic in your approach, and, before you know it, you'll have landed the promotion that you had set your mind on.

Have Confidence

It's easy to become stuck and avoid taking even the first step towards your goal because you lack confidence. Even though you probably have a reasonable track record, this lack of confidence stops you from fulfilling your potential. There will be occasions when you have achieved your goals and some when you haven't. It is worth learning from the experience of an unsuccessful outcome, but there's no point in carrying it with you into your future. Just because you didn't succeed at something in the past does not mean that you will never succeed at it.

> **Minds are like parachutes. They only function when they are open.**
>
> James Dewar

Believe in Yourself

The chances are that you would not bet on yourself being successful at living your dream. This is a test of just how much you believe in yourself. The level of your belief will either propel you forward or stop you thinking about just how great it could be. Having a strong belief in yourself doesn't depend on what other people think of you. It's your opinion about yourself that counts.

- Remember that there never has been another you – you are unique.
- Recognize that you have the same potential as anyone else to do great things.
- Be aware that deep within you hidden talents are waiting to be discovered.
- Have a healthy respect for yourself.

There are many examples of famous people who, against all the odds, have risen above the negative feedback of their parents, teachers, or work colleagues, to become highly successful. The thing they had in common is a strong belief in their own ability. Your lack of belief in your ability to acheive great things may be the only thing stopping you from taking the first step to achieving your goals in life.

Aim High With the right training and equipment you can achieve what you previously thought was impossible.

Effective Affirmations

HIGH IMPACT

- I do my best work when I'm under pressure
- I am confident and engaging before an audience
- I am feeling fit, energetic, and flexible
- I am good at sports and love to learn new things
- I am able to attract all the money I need

NEGATIVE IMPACT

- I always crack when I'm put under pressure
- I'm no good at making presentations
- Now I'm 54, I'm tired and stiff and inflexible
- I am useless at sports, so there's no point in trying
- I don't know why I never seem to have enough money

Build Unconditional Self-Respect

Your sense of self-worth will have been influenced by your parents' limiting and empowering beliefs. However, as an adult, you can choose to believe in yourself and take full responsibility for where you are now. Accept your parents' empowering beliefs about you but discard the influence of your parents' limiting beliefs. There's no point looking back when you are trying to drive your life forward.

Practise Affirmations

Affirmations are simply things that you repeatedly say to yourself. You have been using affirmations all your life, but there's a good chance that they have been negative. To make affirmations work for rather than against you:

- Phrase your message in a way that implies that you are already doing the action in the message.
- Using a positive tone, repeat your message over and over three or four times each day for at least a month.
- If you like, look in the mirror and smile at yourself when you repeat your message.

Eventually, the conscious effort of repeating the affirmation is picked up by your subconscious and you begin to look at your situation in a positive light.

Summary: In the Driving Seat

To be successful, you must put yourself in control of yourself. Recognize how you let obstacles obstruct your progress and explore ways to overcome them. Turn negatives into positives and make the most of every opportunity. Improve your interactive skills by learning more about yourself, building confidence and self-esteem.

Learning to be Positive

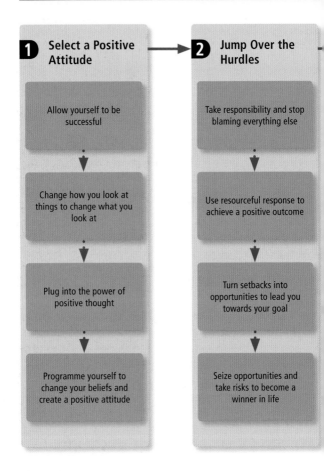

1 Select a Positive Attitude

Allow yourself to be successful

Change how you look at things to change what you look at

Plug into the power of positive thought

Programme yourself to change your beliefs and create a positive attitude

2 Jump Over the Hurdles

Take responsibility and stop blaming everything else

Use resourceful response to achieve a positive outcome

Turn setbacks into opportunities to lead you towards your goal

Seize opportunities and take risks to become a winner in life

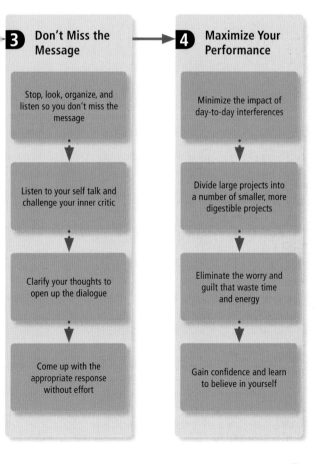

3 **Don't Miss the Message** ➝ **4** **Maximize Your Performance**

Don't Miss the Message	Maximize Your Performance
Stop, look, organize, and listen so you don't miss the message	Minimize the impact of day-to-day interferences
Listen to your self talk and challenge your inner critic	Divide large projects into a number of smaller, more digestible projects
Clarify your thoughts to open up the dialogue	Eliminate the worry and guilt that waste time and energy
Come up with the appropriate response without effort	Gain confidence and learn to believe in yourself

Exercise 4 Your Mind

The more you use your mind, the more effective it becomes. You can stretch your mental muscles to make the most of your mental powers. Practise techniques to increase your memory, find creative solutions, improve your communication skills, and strengthen your performance. This chapter will show you how to:

- Practise ingenious methods for improving your memory
- Think creatively and find ways to uncover previously unconsidered options
- Express yourself clearly
- Use the power of visualization to maximize your performance

Increase Your Memory

One of the easiest ways to increase your memory is to exercise your mind. The traditional memory improvement method was repetition, but this helps very little unless you build in some more powerful strategies.

Use Both Sides of Your Brain

Everyone has a preference towards one side of their brain. If you are more left-brained, you would benefit from working on becoming more creative to help you increase your whole brain approach to thinking and learning. If the right side of your brain is more dominant, you would benefit from more logical learning.

Exercise your mind to keep your memory in peak form

Connect with Your Long-Term Memory

In one ear and out the other is probably the best description of what happens with short-term memory when new information comes in and it is not rehearsed. To help transfer and store the new information in your long-term memory you need to create more connections by adding

think
SMART

There are some things you can do to help you to increase your memory and recall.

Be specific with information – specifics are easier to learn. Take breaks, test and review what you know, and then re-test. Put your new learning into a context, looking at how it fits into the bigger picture. Try to use words that rhyme, memory pegging, and mnemonics. Bring all of your senses into play.

Painting a Picture

Try to memorize the words listed below. You might be able to remember the whole list or a large part of it, but the average score is about 30 per cent.

- tree
- dog
- pencil
- car
- motorway

- money
- traffic lights
- sofa
- cake
- exercise

- chair
- purse
- table
- book
- lake

1 Now read through the list again and, at the same time, create a picture in your mind of each item in turn. Test your recall – there's a good chance that your score will have doubled.

2 Now look at the list again and make each picture more specific. This will help to increase your recall and commit the information to your long-term memory. For example, has your tree got leaves or is it bare? How tall is it? Is it by itself or in a forest? Are there any birds' nests in it? Is it still standing or has it been blown over by the wind? Has someone built a tree house on it?

meaning and a powerful picture in your mind's eye. For example, when you read a book full of information that you need to retain, you will remember more if you take notes as you read each chapter; you will increase your recall even further by cataloguing and categorizing the information. Any deliberate processing of new information will make it more accessible in the future. The simple act of writing down any information you need to remember will impress it more firmly upon your memory; categorizing and cataloguing it will enhance this effect, creating more connections with your long-term memory.

Improve Your Recall

Even if you think you have poor recall, memory pegging will help you to remember a number of unrelated things and recall them in order. It's quite an amusing way to ensure you embed the information to aid recall later. Use this list: 1 = run, 2 = shoe, 3 = ski, 4 = door, 5 = hive, 6 = sticks, 7 = heaven, 8 = plate, 9 = wine, 10 = hen. The first thing to do is to remember the pegs. This should be fairly easy as they all rhyme with the numbers one to ten.

Then create a visual connection that is as humorous and bizarre as possible. For One = Run, conjure up a picture of yourself in a bright pink running kit, with the word you need to remember on top of your head instead of a hat. For Three = Ski, you could be wearing skis instead of running shoes – make them really long and visualize yourself tripping people up. Once you have a strong visual peg, you can use it to memorize lists. This will also help you to remember key aspects of a presentation.

Remembering Lists Try this – think of a familiar journey, "peg" each item on your list to a landmark along it, then replay the route to recall the list.

> **One of the greatest discoveries a man makes, one of his greatest surprises, is to find he can do what he was afraid he couldn't.**
>
> Henry Ford

Use Mnemonics

The simplest and best known example of this type of memory aid is a sentence or phrase where the first letters of each word you want to remember correspond to the first letters of an easily recalled sentence, phrase, or word. Music teachers have traditionally used the mnemonic Every Good Boy Deserves Favour as an aid to remembering one of the basic sequences of notes. It is possible to remember long numbers in a similar way, using the number of letters in each word of a sentence to recall the number. The most famous one is the value of pi – How I wish I could calculate pi (3.141592).

> **Techniques and tricks will improve your recall**

TECHNIQUES
to practise

Another technique to improve your recall is to connect each each item in a list to the next by means of a story told in pictures. Make your story as absurd as possible, as this will make it more memorable.

- Taking your memory list, you might start off with a picture of a bedecked Christmas tree, its lights flashing, in the middle of a muddy field. A brushed and clipped poodle with a blue bow and rhinestone collar is sitting underneath it with a red pencil in its mouth. Finish this story, then recall the list.
- Try the technique with this list: car keys, window, sausages, lightning, coffee, patrol, comb, puppet.
- Use it to exercise your memory, making your own list of random words or names by picking them with a pin from a dictionary or telephone directory.
- On a long car journey with your family, have a list of words that each member in turn has to use to make up their own story.

Be Creative

Being creative is as much about using your imagination as it is about challenging the ways things are done, and then finding a new and better approach.

Think Creatively

When you were a child, you probably used your imagination to come up with lots of ideas for playing games with particular friends or in specific locations, as well as variations on games you'd played before. This creative ability is still within you, although it might take some effort to switch it back on after a long period of disuse. Once you have, you can use it to help you find different solutions for any problems that need solving.

What if...? Thinking

To unlock your creativity and get rid of any roadblocks that prevent you from coming up with different options it is helpful to ask "What if...?" when faced with a problem.

→ Suppose there is a problem in your department that is preventing your organization from making millions.

→ You are trying to come up with some options but have become stuck because of budget constraints, insufficient staff, the wrong machinery, or shortage of time.

→ Turn your thinking around and ask what if you had an adequate budget, enough staff, the right machinery, or sufficient time?

Asking "What if...?" removes any roadblocks that might be stopping you from coming up with answers. It opens up your creative thinking, allowing it to flow without restrictions. Using "What if...?" thinking lets you go anywhere with your thinking.

Recondition Yourself

One of the biggest obstacles to creative thinking is your conditioning. Schools have become aware of this and now use more whole brain learning techniques when teaching children. However, if your education did not follow this approach to learning and thinking, there's a good chance that you will have a left- or right-brain preference, the left being more logical and the right more creative. You may have been told that it is not appropriate to challenge an established view and, over time, you will have become conditioned to accept the way things are done. This type of conditioning removes any real likelihood that you will think "outside the box" and come up with a level of thinking that could transform how you do things in the future. It's never too late to change the way you think about things.

Find New Solutions

Become aware of your conditioning and ask why things are always done in a certain way

Challenge your thinking and develop a more creative, questioning thinking process

Learn to think outside the box to find ways to achieve the results you need

Use your new, creative, and unhampered approach to find creative solutions

Creative Thinking

HIGH IMPACT

- Childlike thinking
- Thinking without restriction
- Thinking your way out of the box
- Thinking big
- Overcoming any roadblocks

NEGATIVE IMPACT

- Closing down opportunities
- Getting stuck at the first hurdle
- Reinforcing your belief that it's not possible
- Thinking small

Accept Change

If a new level of thinking is required for you to come up with a creative solution, you will need to recognize the importance of change as part of the process. You will have to learn how to think differently if you are attempting to change a system that has been in place for a number of years, especially if that system is still working well.

Think Outside the Box

How to look at the bigger picture, or think outside the box, is demonstrated by this exercise known as the Nine Dots.

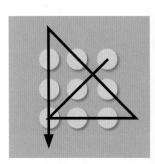

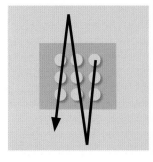

- Copy the pattern of nine dots on to a sheet of paper. Now, join the nine dots with four straight lines without taking your pen off the paper or repeating any lines. Put into the context of performance, you could say that this is what the business expected from you 12 months ago – to be able to connect all of the dots with four straight lines in order to remain competitive in the marketplace.

- Now change the business context. To stay ahead of the

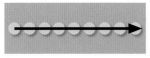

The Nine Dots Use the least number of lines to connect the dots: thinking critically, there is no reason why the lines have to go through the centre of each dot or, more radically, why the dots themselves cannot move.

think
SMART

Looking at ways to manipulate the critical variables of a given situation also works for day-to-day decision-making in your personal life.

Suppose you are thinking about booking the holiday of a lifetime. Variables can include location, mode of transport, type (activity or relaxation), and cost. If you want to visit an exotic location but the cost is too high, think outside the box to see if there is another way to achieve your dream. If time is not an issue could you travel by train instead of by air? Have you considered a working holiday or taking part in a charity event at your chosen destination to make the trip more affordable?

competition you need to join the dots with three straight lines.

- Finally, for the business to stay ahead of the competition and be the industry leader you need to join the dots using only one straight line.

What you learn from doing this exercise is that in order to go from joining the dots with four lines to joining them with one, you have to look at all the critical variables that influence the outcome. These variables are the paper, the pen, and the dots. To come up with the solutions you need to look at how you can manipulate each of these variables: cut the paper, fold the paper, use a fatter pen, make the dots bigger, move the dots. Once you look at the critical variables in any situation, you can apply this thinking to help you come up with solutions to the problem.

Each player must accept the cards life deals him or her; but once they are in hand, he or she alone must decide how to play the cards in order to win the game.

Voltaire

Communicate Better

The quality of your communication can be assessed by the response to what you have said. If communication is poor, then you cannot expect people to get the point.

Top Ten Tips for Talking

There are some simple rules to follow, whether you are talking to one person or a group.

- You should know what you want to say.
- You should believe in your message.
- You should know what the listener wants to hear.

It is also important to:

- Be aware of the key messages and outcomes.
- Avoid jargon.
- Use gestures and make eye contact.
- Use pace, pause, volume, speed, and emphasis.
- Ask questions.
- Inject some humour.
- Use stories and anecdotes.

In a business presentation, you could use music, flip charts, and other props to make it more memorable. Make sure you get the pre-frame (the summary of what you're going to talk about) right.

Use Humour If it's appropriate, inject some fun into your presentation. It will help people remember you next time.

Be Crystal Clear

Lack of clarity is the main obstacle to effective communication. Even if you think that you have put your point across properly, if your audience is confused, it won't know what to make of what you have just shared.

It is essential to deliver the message to your target audience in their language. This is not about speaking French or Italian, but about using words and examples the listener can relate to.

We all have preferred ways of giving and receiving information. The three most common are visual, auditory, and kinaesthetic. Everyday examples of these are:

→ **Visual** – "If you look at this next slide, you'll be able to see the big picture."

→ **Auditory** – "You obviously can't hear what I'm saying; I thought that you liked the sound of this."

→ **Kinaesthetic** – "I sense that you're not sure about this."

Common Figures of Speech

VISUAL (SEEING)	AUDITORY (HEARING)	KINAESTHETIC
• Beyond a shadow of a doubt	• Can't hear myself think	• He's a bit slippery
• Bird's-eye view	• Clear as a bell	• This is weighing me down
• Can't see it	• Hold your tongue	• I'm feeling low
• Eye to eye	• Loud and clear	• I sense you're not happy
• In light of	• Slip of the tongue	• I've got a gut feeling
• Mind's eye	• Sounds good	• I'm immersed in this game
• Paint a picture	• That doesn't sound right	
• Picture this	• Really off beat	• This band is really hot
• Shed some light on	• It's screaming out for a solution	• The pressure's on
• Sight for sore eyes		• He's on fire
• For your eyes only	• I hear what you say	• She's got the world on her shoulders
• See the big picture	• Music to my ears	
• Seeing is believing		

Discover the Referencing

Whether someone is internally or externally referenced is another useful thing to be aware of when you are talking to them or giving them feedback. Internally referenced people will have an opinion about themselves and how well they are doing at a task. They will probably have strong inner guidance, and will be less inclined to rely on feedback from others.

- An internally referenced person willingly answers questions about how she thinks she has performed a task, what has worked well, and where she thinks she can improve.
- She will not respond well to being told what other people think of her performance. Even if the feedback is positive, she'll be inclined to think you are just trying to make her feel good.

Externally referenced people rely more on feedback from others to assure them of their performance. They can fall into the trap of becoming dependent on constant feedback to make them feel better.

- An externally referenced person will want to hear what others think about her performance.
- She will feel uncomfortable if asked to assess her performance due to her concern about what others think.

5 minute FIX

At the next team meeting, pay attention to the language being used by each individual.

- List their names and check whether they are internally or externally referenced.
- Give them a V = Visual, A = Auditory, or K = Kinaesthetic depending on the words they use.

Get the Pre-Frame Right

Whether you are going to deliver some difficult feedback to a team member or are about to speak at a conference, pre-framing is critical to achieving your desired outcome. The pre-frame is a summary of what you are going to talk about. It sets the scene so that everyone knows where you are going and may include some signposts to show how you are going to get there. Scene-setting makes people feel more comfortable as they know where you are going. Pre-framing also provides you with a structure for your presentation or feedback so that you are clear about what you are going to say and what your key messages are.

Enhance Your Interactions

The great presenters and communicators in all walks of life offer clues about how to get your message across well. A certain newscaster or comedian might have a style or mannerism that you can draw on. You can also look for tips in books. If you apply the win, learn, change strategy (geared at finding out what were your wins, learns from a project or event and then applying any changes to help you achieve a better outcome next time) and write down quotes, you can try them out at the next opportunity.

TIP Make sure that you set aside enough time to pre-frame. Focusing on the outcome you want will help you to get the pre-frame right.

Use the Power of Visualization

In 1954, Roger Bannister became the first person to break the four-minute mile barrier. He had seen himself achieve this record in his mind's eye hundreds of times.

Work Your Imagination

Imagine holding a ripe lemon with a waxy feel to the skin. You cut it in half with a sharp knife and squeeze the juice all over a salad. As you do this, you can smell the distinctive citrus aroma, and you decide to bite into the flesh to quench your thirst. As you bite into

Visualize success in order to succeed

the lemon, the smell becomes even stronger and juice drips from the corners of your mouth. While you were reading this, did you find yourself salivating to try and get rid of the lemon taste in your mouth? If you did, you have just used your imagination to re-create an actual event. By

CASE study: Creating a New Picture

Natalie had tried to stop smoking many times. Frustrated by her "weak-mindedness", she consulted her cousin Holly who had successfully given up some months earlier. Holly suggested that instead of focusing on the harm smoking does, she should focus on the benefits of quitting. Natalie settled on a date to quit, and for a week before she visualized being a non-smoker. She smelled the freshness of her hair and breath, felt the smoothness of the skin around her eyes and mouth, saw her hands and teeth free of nicotine stains. Quitting day came and Natalie put her plan into action. Every time she craved a cigarette, she visualized herself as a non-smoker.

• *By "seeing" what life would be like without cigarettes Natalie was able to find the strength and determination to give them up.*
• *After six weeks, she had her teeth polished and joined a gym.*
• *After a year without cigarettes she is fitter and healthier, and has a new interest in good food.*

learning how to heighten all your senses through visualization, you can

Visualize Your Goal View your goal from different perpsectives – from your own and from those who observe you.

reproduce some very powerful results while sitting in your armchair in the comfort of your own home.

Rehearse Mentally

Mental rehearsal has become the norm for top performers in every field. Research has produced some amazing evidence of how powerful this technique is.

- Using modern scanning imagery, researchers have observed what happens when someone is wired up and performs the simple task of running around a basketball court. They could see which muscles were being fired to help the runner get from A to B and back again.
- Using the same scanning equipment and with the electrodes in place, researchers asked the volunteer to visualize doing the same exercise. They could see the same muscles being fired off in the same sequence.

Visualize Success

Suppose you have an important presentation to make and you've never made one to such a large group before. You can use visualization to go through the whole process in your mind's eye. Your visualization will include some of the following: your journey to the venue; the clothes you are going to wear; the people you will have met during the course of the day; the layout of the room; the appearance of the audience – smart or casual dress; the time of day; the stories you are going to tell; how you will be feeling. You will probably also visualize:

- The person who will introduce you
- The type of microphone – hand-held or lapel
- The visual aids you will use – slides and other media
- The order in which you are going to use the visual aids.

Once you are at the venue, you can sit in the auditorium and visualize yourself standing on the stage, making your introduction confidently and proceeding to give an excellent presentation to a receptive and enthusiastic audience.

Train Your Mind

You can train your mind to deal with any kind of adverse situation by visualizing a positive outcome. Athletes who manage pain during endurance events, such as a marathon, can fool their minds that it's not so bad as the signals being sent to the brain suggest. In the build-up for training for a marathon, athletes will do some longer, more punishing runs. The more training of this kind they do beforehand, the better prepared they will be to manage any pain that they experience on race day.

5 minute FIX

If you write "to do" lists, but never take action, try visualization.

- Look at your list, prioritize, and focus on the first item.
- Visualize each step of carrying out the action.
- Visualize the positive outcome.
- Visualize yourself, having achieved the positive outcome.

Get in the Zone

Imagine you are waiting to be called for the final of the 100m at an important race meeting. You've done your pre-race stretching and warm-ups, you've eaten at the right time to ensure that you are fuelled, and you're ready to go.

When the announcer introduces your event, you feel great – you are in the zone. This is the first time you've got this far at a track event, yet you have already run this race thousands of times in your mind. Your visualization will have addressed the following:

→ How long will you have to wait before the race starts?
→ Which lane will you be starting from?
→ Who is going to be in the race? Who is going to be running alongside you?
→ What is the weather going to be like?
→ What is the noise from the crowd going to be like? What other noises will you hear?
→ What is a full stadium going to look like?
→ What smells will you smell?
→ What pre-race routine will you go through now that you are in the stadium?
→ What will it feel like to win the race?

The more vividly you can create an image of success using visualization, the better chance you have of winning. If you are looking for a competitive edge, mental rehearsal will help embed the unfamilar into being familar. The more you practise visualization, the quicker it will become part of your normal routine.

Use Visualization

Visualize Your Success

⬇

Visualize the place where you will perform

⬇

Focus on your preparation and props

⬇

See yourself achieving success/winning

Summary: Stretching Your Mind

Hone your mind through simple exercises that can then be employed as useful strategies in real situations. Increase the power of your memory, discover how to think outside the box and solve "insoluble" problems, master the art of successful communication, and mobilize visualization techniques to think your way to success.

Optimize the Power of Your Mind

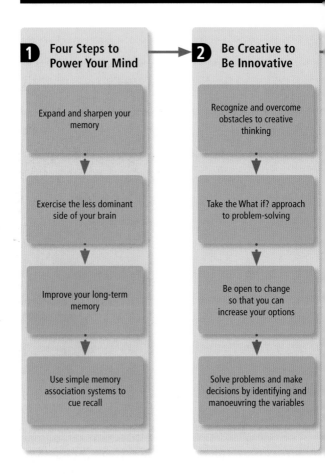

1 Four Steps to Power Your Mind

Expand and sharpen your memory

↓

Exercise the less dominant side of your brain

↓

Improve your long-term memory

↓

Use simple memory association systems to cue recall

2 Be Creative to Be Innovative

Recognize and overcome obstacles to creative thinking

↓

Take the What if? approach to problem-solving

↓

Be open to change so that you can increase your options

↓

Solve problems and make decisions by identifying and manoeuvring the variables

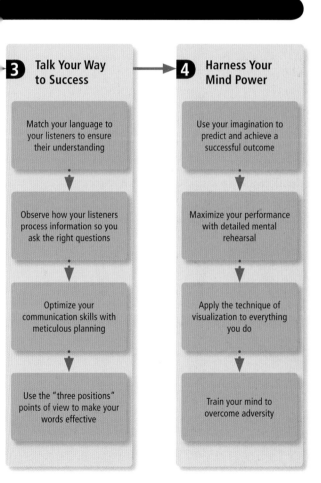

3 **Talk Your Way to Success**

Match your language to your listeners to ensure their understanding

Observe how your listeners process information so you ask the right questions

Optimize your communication skills with meticulous planning

Use the "three positions" points of view to make your words effective

4 **Harness Your Mind Power**

Use your imagination to predict and achieve a successful outcome

Maximize your performance with detailed mental rehearsal

Apply the technique of visualization to everything you do

Train your mind to overcome adversity

Mind Over 5
Matter

Knowing whether your mind runs you or you run your mind is what this book is about. This last chapter will help you to discover what you want, and how to coach yourself to get the outcomes you desire. It also looks at interacting with and influencing others, together with becoming more aware of how important it is to use the right words. You will find out how to:

- Use dynamic language to energize and motivate yourself and others
- Find your purpose, then organize your life so that you can live your dream
- Be your own performance coach
- Create the right impression and have a positive impact on everyone you meet

The Power of Words

Misunderstandings often arise from the way words are used and the meanings that become attached to them. If you can improve your use of words, you will be able to communicate more clearly.

Focus on What You Want

When you focus on what you want, you usually get it. It's also true that when you focus on what you don't want, you usually get it. Recognizing that you are focusing on what you don't want is difficult.

Use Positive Language

Your mind is a powerful tool that struggles to relate to the negative aspects of words. It's so powerful that it deletes the negative from a statement and sets to work on helping you in a positive tone. For example, suppose you said to yourself, "I don't want to miss my next sales target." Your mind deletes the "don't" aspect of the apparently negative thought and you are left with the apparently positive, "I want to miss my next sales target." To put yourself in the best possible position to hit your sales target, focus

Positive Approach Encourage individuals and groups to perform at their best by focusing on what's going well and using positive language.

your language on the positive. Say to yourself, "I want to hit my next sales target" or, better still, "I will hit my next sales target."

Understand Different Meanings

When Americans ask "Would you like to wash up?", they are offering you the opportunity to wash your hands before having dinner. This has caused confusion among many non-Americans who wash up – do the dishes – after dinner. Avoid being misunderstood in a cross-cultural context by being more aware of how words and phrases are used in different ways.

5 minute FIX

If you're feeling really negative about a difficult situation at work, try to get yourself into a positive frame of mind.

- Think about how you would feel if everything was going smoothly.
- Practise telling people how well it's going, and why.

TECHNIQUES *to* practise

Try to respond positively when someone asks you how you are. Common responses are: "okay" or "could be worse". These stock replies are neither energizing nor uplifting and will affect your mood and that of the other person. Use energizing replies when you are feeling a little low. Your mind is very clever at focusing on the positive and will trigger the release of endorphins, making you feel better.

- Make a conscious effort to make positive responses to people for a week.
- Tell them that you're "brilliant", "fantastic", "really excited", "really well", "having a great day", "on top of the world". Say that you just "couldn't be better".
- Check what sort of effect these replies have on how you are actually feeling. The chances are that will you start to feel better almost immediately.

Know What You Want

If you were to ask anyone what they wanted from life, you might be surprised to find that most people will struggle to list what they want to do, to be, and to have. A sense of purpose gives meaning to your life.

What's Your Purpose?

Have you ever asked yourself what it's all about? Why have you showed up here? Why are you here now? Is there something you're meant to be doing? Shouldn't there be more to life than this? You are not alone in pondering these questions, and they are good questions to think about. You are here for a purpose. If you haven't found your hidden talent yet, then it's worth spending time thinking about what you should be doing.

- Your purpose is something that energizes you, gets you involved in things you really enjoy doing.
- When you are living your purpose, your life is effortless and everything you do seems easy.
- When you are living your purpose, even when you are knocked back, you find it easy just to get up, dust yourself off, and carry on with what you were doing.

think
SMART

However busy you feel, taking a little time to analyze what is important to you will help you to organize your time better. It is easy to dismiss the idea of balance in your life on the grounds that you have no control over the demands on your time.

Knowing what is neither pressing nor important can free up time for you to learn a foreign language or play chess with your son or daughter. In the light of this, refuse to take on any more non-essential or unimportant commitments and use the time that you save for whatever is important to you.

Find Your Purpose

Going Nowhere? If you feel that you're on a treadmill, perhaps the time has come to find your purpose in life.

Do you remember what you loved doing when you were growing up? What was it that absorbed you so completely that you just lost all track of time? Did you then just bumble along from school to university to your first job – and have you ended up now with a CV and a career based on chasing the next promotion? Many people do. Most of the time this is an ego-driven decision that continues to take you further away from your purpose and helps bury your hidden talent. Perhaps you no longer know what your purpose is. The closer you can get to doing something that nourishes your heart and a job that you love, the closer you will be to finding your purpose.

TIP If you're struggling to find your purpose, go on-line, visit a library, speak to your friends, or attend a seminar on a subject that interests you.

Get the Order Right

There are three main aspects of your life to get in order. These are self, family, and work. You need to place them in some sort of hierarchy based on how much attention you give to each aspect. If you have a busy job, you will probably put work first because you think that you devote most time and energy to it. That might be true, particularly if you carry on working after you've got home, when you could be pursuing a hobby or spending time with your family.

Use the Wheel to Plan Your Life

Once you have placed self, family, and work in order (be honest about where your time and energy are currently allocated), you can then take a closer look at your life. Use the wheel to help you gain clarity in all three areas of your

Family Wheel

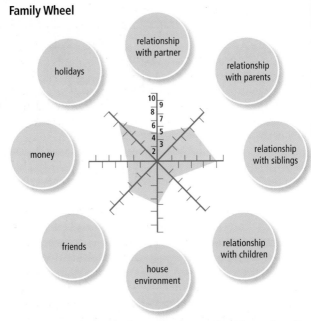

Visualize Your Values Give yourself a score from 1-10 for each area of your life, where 1 = least amount of fulfilment and 10 = most amount of fulfilment.

The Farewell Party

Finding and living your purpose and prioritizing the main aspects of your life will not happen overnight and, even when you are getting there, things can still slip. To sharpen your focus, try playing the farewell party game.

Imagine that you are emigrating to the other side of the world and throwing a farewell party at which speeches are made.

→ What would you most like to hear a member of your immediate family say about you?
→ What would you most like to hear a close friend or relative say about you?
→ What would you most like to hear one of your colleagues say about you?
→ What would you say yourself, if asked to speak?

Doing this exercise will help you to recognize what sort of person you really want to be. You are not defining yourself in others' terms, but teasing out your idea of who you want to be. Wouldn't you rather be "fun to be with" rather than "never any trouble as a neighbour", or "a great team player" rather than "the person who always stayed late to finish the filing"?

life – a family wheel is shown opposite, and you can adapt this model to create wheels for self and work. Once you've filled out each wheel with your scores, you can see where you are now in each area of your life compared to where you want to be. Using the three wheels, you can make a separate plan for each of the three main parts of your life and apply a timescale for achieving each of your goals. For each of the points on the wheel you can map out the steps you will need to take in order to increase each one to a 10.

Coach Yourself

An open mind will enable you to learn more quickly and move towards your goals more rapidly. Having an open mind will change your life for the better.

Use a Journal to Keep Score

Getting into the habit of using a journal to monitor various aspects of your life and using this as a way to unravel patterns of behaviour, listing your goals, and writing down your thoughts is a powerful tool. It provides a snapshot of what you were thinking at different times and helps you to remember key aspects of your life. It also helps to relieve stress. Simply writing things down means that you will carry around less of your story, which can weigh you down. If you write down your goals, you are more likely to achieve them.

Starting Your Journal

Spend some time choosing a journal that you like. There's no point in buying a large format journal if you are going to carry it with you most of the time. Some people jot down their thoughts in a small notebook and expand them later in a larger journal. There are no rules for what goes into your journal and you can keep separate journals for your work and home lives. If you like, ask other people, such as your children, to contribute to one of your journals.

5 minute FIX

Make writing your journal part of your routine by setting aside a special time.

- Decide on the best time to write up your journal – it might be last thing at night or while commuting to or from work.

- Schedule it into your diary until it becomes a matter of habit.

> **Some men see things as they are and say "Why?" I dream things that never were and say "Why not?"**
>
> George Bernard Shaw

Focus on What you Can Do

It's easy to get derailed from focusing on your goals; everyday life means squeezing a lot into a single day. While it's easy to find excuses for not doing something, it's just as easy to find reasons for doing it. Imagine that you are on your way from London to a meeting in Paris early the next morning and your flight (the last flight of the day) is cancelled. If you're feeling negative you'll probably decide to cancel the meeting. Look for the alternatives: you can probably take a train and still get to the meeting on time, or take a taxi to another airport and fly from there. When you start focusing on what you can do, it makes you aware of options that you might not have thought of previously. Unfortunately, it's all too easy to focus on what you don't want.

An open mind will show what you can achieve

TECHNIQUES *to* practise

When you find yourself going through a bad patch or just not feeling good about yourself, try writing an alternative journal.

- Divide each page into three columns. In the first column, write down the event, conversation, decision, situation, or whatever it is that has triggered your negative thoughts and feelings.

- Write down these thoughts and feelings in the second column of your journal.

- Find positive thoughts and feelings that could have been triggered by the entry in the first column and write these down in the third column.

- Next time you experience a negative response to an event look at the third column in your journal to find an alternative, positive reaction.

CASE study: Telling the Truth to Be Kind

Ramesh was a successful sales manager, well liked by the team that reported to him. However, his hopes of promotion remained unfulfilled. He was efficient, had a great track record, and always hit his sales targets. His one weakness was the quality of his presentations at national conferences. More was expected of someone at his level within the business. His manager made comforting comments, such as "The audience was difficult"; "You had to cut your presentation because everyone else had overrun"; "You got the main points across". Eventually, a new manager was appointed. She had a lot of experience in making presentations at large meetings and was able to give Ramesh constructive feedback about his presenting skills. The feedback accelerated his career.

- *Ramesh's career had hit a plateau because his manager had never given him the feedback he needed. Comments were never specific enough for him to improve his performance.*
- *Once his new manager provided the right feedback, Ramesh was able to focus his effort and energy into doing a stunning job the next time he got the opportunity.*

Tell the Truth

When you were a child, you were so innocent that you always told the truth, until you realized that you might get away with holding back some of it to save yourself from getting into trouble. In reality, telling lies or withholding the full story doesn't usually get you out of trouble. In most cases, it gets you further into trouble and then you find yourself in a situation where you have to explain why you've been trying to cover things up.

Use Diplomacy

Being too diplomatic is a form of failing to tell the truth and is one that is often utilized in the workplace. You can end up not giving someone the help they need because you think that they might not be able to handle the truth. Use your skills of diplomacy to tell people the truth in a way that doesn't shatter their self-confidence yet encourages them to improve their performance to achieve better results in future. Diplomacy is about being sensitive and appropriate to every interaction.

Seek the Truth

If you have a reputation for being a truthful person, it puts you in a strong position to ask others for truthful feedback. One of the best ways to get closer to the truth is to ask for feedback. Get one of your colleagues to look out for occasions when you do the very thing that you are focused on changing. When others are providing feedback, ask them to be specific. If someone says that you did a good job, ask them to pinpoint what they were most pleased with and where there is room for improvement.

Dynamic Feedback Just as a conductor will draw out the best in individual performers, there are times when you should trust others to be the judge of your performance.

Model Excellence

If you want to start a new business, but have little experience in running one, identify someone in your local community who has done something similar and invite him out to lunch. You might be surprised at how easy it is to find out how he started out and what he learned along the way. Armed with knowledge of the pitfalls you will be better prepared and able to navigate your way around your first successful year in your own business.

Reveal Your Strengths

If you had a performance coach to help you achieve your goals, he would start from the belief that you already have the solutions to the things that are challenging you or preventing you from achieving your dreams. He will ask you penetrating questions to help focus your attention on getting what you want. A good coach will not let you off with any excuses. He will help to keep you focused towards your goals.

5 minute FIX

Spend a brief period each day on enhancing your strengths.

- Read more books in your chosen field.
- Listen to CDs or tapes by experts.
- Reflect on your day and what went well.

Use Your Resources

You rarely need to look outside the network of friends and business contacts you already have to help you achieve your goals. All the resources you might need are usually already within your grasp. It's just that you haven't previously concentrated on looking for them. When you become aware of what it is you want to achieve, you'll be in a better position to target the things and people you need to realize your aims and ambitions.

TIP Show an interest in the people in your current network so that they will be there to offer support when you are in need of their help.

A Virtual Board of Directors

Behind every successful company is a strong board of directors who pool their talents and help steer the company through challenging times. They have the ability to ensure that the business goes from strength to strength.

Form your own imaginary board of directors to help you with the tricky business decisions you might have to make. You can draw on their thinking when you are faced with anything that troubles you. The people you choose can be real or fictitious, dead or alive.

Once you have your board of directors, you can tap into their thinking and ask yourself what they would have done in your situation. If they have made it on to your board, you'll know enough about them to know how they would respond to particular situations. Draw on them whenever you need to.

Choose Your Heroes

HISTORICAL FIGURES

- **Artists** – Michelangelo, Vermeer
- **Inventors** – Thomas Edison, Leonardo Da Vinci
- **Military leaders** – Alexander the Great, Joan of Arc
- **Political leaders** – Mahatma Gandhi, Winston Churchill
- **Writers** – Rumi, Helen Keller

PUBLIC FIGURES

- **Business leaders** – Henry Ford, Andrew Carnegie
- **Entrepreneurs** – Richard Branson, Bill Gates
- **Scientists** – Alexander Fleming, Marie Curie
- **Sporting heroes** – Muhammad Ali, Lance Armstrong

FICTITIOUS FIGURES

- **Cartoon characters** – Batman, the Pink Panther
- **Characters from films, books, and plays** – Rocky, Sydney Carton (from Charles Dickens' *A Tale of Two Cities*), Portia (from William Shakespeare's *The Merchant of Venice*)

PERSONAL HEROES

- **Family members**
- **Former bosses**
- **Current boss**
- **Friends**
- **Relatives**
- **Mentors**
- **Inspiring public figure**
- **Favourite teacher**

Interact with Others

Living in this chaotic world, you are probably unaware of how much society has shaped your thinking and how this impacts on the way you interact with everyone with whom you come into contact.

Let Go of Being Right

The need to be right can cause you many problems. If you dig your heels in you will not pay proper attention to another person's perspective. The best way to ensure you achieve rapport with someone is to be able to see and hear his or her point of view. If you don't agree with that point of view, just ask more questions to gain a deeper understanding of his opinions and greater clarity about where and how he formed them. Approach every conversation from a position of not having to be right, and know that you are only ever one conversation away from resolving any challenging situation. This will help you to interact effectively with others.

> **You cannot find a remedy simply by condemning something**

What's in a Name?

How do you feel when someone has forgotten your name? You are not alone if it makes you feel a little less important and significant. Successful business leaders ensure that they know the names of everyone they will meet when visiting a site away from head office. They obtain background information about the staff they will be meeting in advance so that they are well prepared. You can do the same before your meetings. If you meet ten new people at a training day, avoid introducing yourself to everyone at once and trying to remember their names – you won't be able to keep them all in your head. Start by talking to a couple of people, embed their names in your memory, then move on to the next two people.

Creating a Positive First Impression

First impressions count, so you need to get it right first time. In addition to dressing appropriately and paying attention to your appearance, make sure your body language reinforces the impression you want to create.

Make Eye Contact
Establishing good eye contact for a couple of seconds helps to convey honesty and openness – if you are excited this will also show up in your eyes. Don't overdo it though because it can become intrusive.

Remember to Smile
However nervous or worried you are, greeting someone with an infectious smile makes a brilliant first impression. A smile immediately creates a bond between you and the person you are meeting.

Establish Physical Contact We've all experienced a bad handshake, from limp and insipid ones to bone-crushers, and the memory tends to stay with us. Be in control of making a confident first contact.

Be Positive

When you start a conversation with someone, it's important to begin with things that you can both agree about. Focus on starting with a positive intention so that the dynamic allows the conversation to go with the flow.

- If you start with something contentious, it is difficult to establish a rapport. Having said no to some point, you will go on to defend your no. In such a situation you tend to do your utmost to avoid backing down.
- Getting into a pattern of yes, yes, yes has a completely different psychology. The person you're talking to will feel calmer and more relaxed, and will already be disposed to saying yes. This will make it easier for him to remain in agreement with you.

The best way to start a conversation is to start with a topic that is safe and uncontroversial. Then, depending on whether the response you get is positive or negative, you can formulate your next question. This is a subtle process that doesn't involve firing off a raft of questions.

TECHNIQUES *to* practise

If you tend to forget people's names, use this technique when you meet someone new to embed his name in your memory.

1 When you meet someone for the first time at a party, spend some time talking to him. Use his name a few times during the conversation, trying not to sound unnatural. Then repeat his name one last time when you say goodbye at the end of the evening.

2 Find out something about the person and attach that piece of information to his name in your mind – Steve with the staring eyes or Sam with the six children.

3 Test yourself with your partner or your host to make sure you've got the name right.

4 If you are attending a business meeting, draw a seating plan and fill in the names of people when they are mentioned in the conversation.

CASE study: Getting It into the Open

Tracey and James have been living together for a number of years. James is the better cook, so whenever they have friends over for dinner he's the king of the kitchen. He's always made it clear that he needs space and solitude while he's cooking, and Tracey keeps out of his way while she organizes the table settings and the drinks, and cleans the house before their guests arrive. When their guests leave, James goes to bed, leaving Tracey to do the cleaning up. James has never spoken about his expectation that she will do the cleaning up, and is very surprised when she voices her resentment. He had understood that his expectation was a given in their relationship. They agreed on a compromise – James would do the dishes, while Tracey would clear up the dining room.

• *By stating his rules but failing to make his expectations clear, James put his relationship with Tracey under pressure due to the lack of clarity.*
• *Once his expectations had been discussed they were able to agree on a way forward that was acceptable to both of them.*
• *This opened up a healthy conversation about other aspects of their relationship and they were both more aware of each other's rules and expectations.*

Be Aware of Rules and Expectations

Many relationships suffer because people do not share their rules and expectations. The parties in a relationship need an understanding of what the rules are and what is considered to be acceptable behaviour within the context of the relationship. Most organizations now realize the importance of making sure that everyone is aware of the framework within which they should be operating. Those organizations that tend to leave their staff in the dark about what is expected of them usually have a poor record of staff retention and will spend a lot of time recruiting new people for their teams. If your personal relationships are to succeed and flourish, you will need to share your rules and expectations with those concerned.

Summary: Empowering Your Mind

Use your mind to drive your life forward to the place where you really want to be. Discover how forceful words are, and use that force to positive effect. Find out what you really want and set about achieving it. Use your mental powers to train yourself to reach your goals. Understand how you interact with others and enhance your impact.

Expand Your Potential

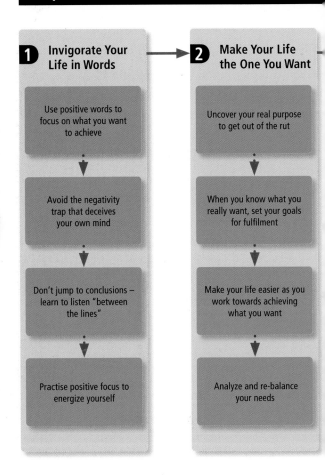

1 Invigorate Your Life in Words

- Use positive words to focus on what you want to achieve
- Avoid the negativity trap that deceives your own mind
- Don't jump to conclusions – learn to listen "between the lines"
- Practise positive focus to energize yourself

2 Make Your Life the One You Want

- Uncover your real purpose to get out of the rut
- When you know what you really want, set your goals for fulfilment
- Make your life easier as you work towards achieving what you want
- Analyze and re-balance your needs

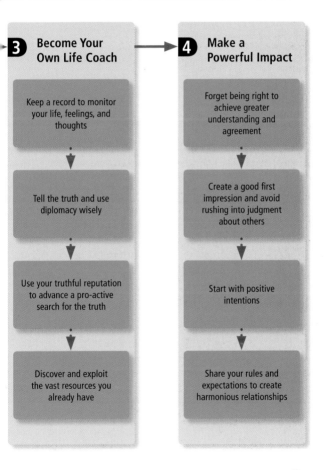

3 Become Your Own Life Coach

Keep a record to monitor your life, feelings, and thoughts

↓

Tell the truth and use diplomacy wisely

↓

Use your truthful reputation to advance a pro-active search for the truth

↓

Discover and exploit the vast resources you already have

4 Make a Powerful Impact

Forget being right to achieve greater understanding and agreement

↓

Create a good first impression and avoid rushing into judgment about others

↓

Start with positive intentions

↓

Share your rules and expectations to create harmonious relationships

Index

Picture Credits

The publisher would like to thank the following for their kind permission to reproduce their photographs: Abbreviations key: (l) = left, (c) = centre, (r) = right, (t) = top, (b) = below, (cl) = centre left, (cr) = centre right.

1: Chris Cole/Iconica/Getty (l), Eileen Bach/Riser/Getty (c), Michael Touraine/Jupiter Images (r); **2:** Justin Pumfrey/Iconica/Getty **3:** Bruce Laurance/Taxi/Getty (t), VEER Florian Franke/Photonica/Getty (c), Stuart O'Sullivan/The Image Bank/Getty (b); **5:** Yellow Dog Productions/The Image Bank/Getty; **7:** Bernard van Berg/Iconica/Getty; **8:** Roberto Mettifogo/Photonica/Getty (l), Michel Touraine/Jupiter Images (cl), Photolibrarycom/Photonica/Getty (cr), Manfred Rutz/Photonica/Getty (r); **13:** Ron Chapple/Taxi/Getty; **14:** China Tourism Press/The Image Bank/Getty; **16:** Brian Bailey/Stone/Getty; **22:** VEER John Churchman/Photonica/Getty; **25:** Photolibrarycom/Photonica/Getty; **27:** Tom Stock/The Image Bank/Getty; **29:** Ronald Rammelkamp/FoodPix/Jupiter Images; **33:** Bernard van Berg/Iconica/Getty; **36:** VEER Florian Franke/Photonica/Getty; **42:** Chris Cole/Iconica/Getty; **49:** Nathan Bilow/Allsport Concepts/Getty; **55:** Peter Newton/Stone/Getty; **56:** PunchStock; **59:** Simon Watson/The Image Ban/Getty; **63:** Bill Losh/Taxi/Getty; **65:** Manfred Rutz/Photonica/Getty; **69:** Michael Hemsley; **70:** Michael Touraine/Jupiter Images; **74:** Tom Stock/The Image Bank/Getty; **77:** Ulli Seer/Stone/Getty; **79:** Antonio M Rosario/The Image Bank/Getty; **82:** Eileen Bach/Riser/Getty; **88:** Anne Rippy/Iconica/Getty; **93:** Yukihiro Fukuda/Orion Press/Jupiter Images; **97:** Bernard van Berg/IconicaGetty; **99:** Roberto Mettifogo/Photonica/Getty; **100:** Nathan Billow/Allsport Concepts/Getty; **103:** Bruce Laurance/Taxi/Getty; **109:** Chad Ehlers/Stock Connection/Jupiter Images; **113:** Michael Hemsley; **117:** Yellow Dog Productions/The Image Bank/Getty.

All other images © Dorling Kindersley.

For further information see www.dkimages.com

Author's Acknowledgments

This has been a great learning experience for me, I have been amazed to see what goes into bringing a book to life from behind the scenes. Thank you to all of the editorial team, Adèle Hayward, Simon Tuite, Fiona Biggs, Tim Jollands and Terry Jeavons for all of the support. A big thanks to all of my teachers, especially the ones who live with me.

Author's Biography

Jim Rees is Managing Director of Ripple Leadership Ltd, a company that focuses on maximizing potential at individual, team, and organizational levels, working with many FTSE 100 companies across Europe. At 16 he became the youngest ethical buyer in Australia and then spent 13 years in sales and sales management in the pharmaceutical industry. Jim combines being a parent of six children with his business and sporting careers, which include numerous Ironman Triathlons around the world and, more recently, the Race Across America in 2005 as captain of Team Inspiration. Jim believes that we are all built for greatness, and, as an author, keynote speaker, and performance coach he's doing everything he can to prove it.